Hebrew Academy of West Queens

The Hebrew Academy of [...] lished to perpetuate the [...] ur heritage, to teach Torah to o[...] so that they will have both the inspiration and understanding to live as observant Jews. From its inception, the Yeshiva has been in the forefront of the "kiruv" movement, igniting the flame of Yiddishkeit in thousands of American public school and immigrant children who would have been lost to assimilation.

Over the past twenty-six years, the school has provided thousands of these children with a Torah true education. Its graduates have become outstanding students in many of the well-known Yeshiva institutions. The two-hundred and fifty students currently enrolled in the Yeshiva in Jackson Heights come from neighborhoods throughout Queens.

What distinguishes the Hebrew Academy of West Queens from Yeshivas that cater exclusively to immigrant children? At the Hebrew Academy immigrant children are placed in a setting where they interact with and learn from veteran Yeshiva students. Immigrant students who have already become Torah oriented have a very positive effect on new arrivals. The Yeshiva and its dedicated staff impart our heritage in an environment where both the advanced and beginning students from all backgrounds and cultures can flourish.

34-25 82nd Street / Jackson Heights N.Y. 11372 / (718) 899-9193

Best wishes for a

שנה טובה ומתוקה

From the Staff
and Students of

Hebrew Academy
of West Queens

In Loving Memory

of

Our Dear Parents

Joseph and Fanny Leitner

ר׳ יוסף בן ר׳ יעקב ז״ל

נפטר י״ט ניסן תשמ״ב

מרת פייגא בת ר׳ יעקב ע״ה

נפטרה ערב ראש השנה – כ״ט אלול תש״ן

Their Lifelong Dedication
to Torah Education
Continues to be an Inspiration to us
Their Children and Grandchildren

❧❦❧

Mr. and Mrs. Herbert Somerstein and Family
Rabbi and Mrs. Moshe Stahler and Family
Mr. and Mrs. Shlomo Orbach and Family
Mr. and Mrs. Steven Prager and Family
Dr. and Mrs. Harry Kaplovitz and Family

In Memory of

Benjamin Solkoff ע״ה

and

Paul Ledet ע״ה

Irving and Arlene Solkoff

David and Elycia

Sam Gold

Rose Solkoff

Dora Ledet

Leslie Ledet

Joseph and Judy Marmo

Daniel and Bonnie

In Memory of

Emily and Nathan Selengut ע״ה

Eda and S.J. Weisberger ע״ה

Leonard Stahler ע״ה

Whose love, wisdom and teachings
will be with us always

Esti and Ushi Stahler
and Family

לזכר נשמת

אבא מורי

אברהם אבא בן אהרן אליעזר ע״ה

אמא מורתי

האשה חיה בת דוד הכהן ע״ה

סקאלער

לזכר נשמת

מרדכי בן ר׳ שמואל העבט ע״ה

In memory of

Max Hecht

מאת המשפחה

In Memory of

Morris and Anna Hulkower

Louis and Rose Zyniewski

Lee Zyniewski

Libby Alperowitz

Helen Goodman

לזכר נשמות

ר׳ משה אהרן בן דוד הלוי ע״ה

ר׳ יודעל בן משה ע״ה

אסנא מכלא בת עזר ע״ה

ר׳ משה בן יהודה יודעל ע״ה

מלכה בת מרדכי ע״ה

אהרן מיכל בן משה ע״ה

In Memory of

Morris Zharnest

Joseph Kline

Alice Kline

Morris Kline

Mollie Kline

Aaron Ehrenberg

❧❦❧

David and Frumi Ehrenberg
Baila, Yitzchak, Naftali and Malka

לזכר נשמות

חיה בת ר׳ אליעזר הלוי סראלאוויטש

ר׳ נפתלי בן ר׳ רפאל פרוידינבערגער

אסתר בת ר׳ יחיאל מיכל ווינקלער

May their exemplary lives of devotion to Torah

and chesed be an inspiration to their children,

grandchildren and great grandchildren

❧❦❧

Mr. and Mrs. Allen Szrolovits

and Family

לזכר נשמות

אבי מורי

ר' חיים יהושע
ב"ר דוד ע"ה

אחותי היקרה
האשה שרה פייגא
בת ר' חיים יהושע ע"ה

In Memory of

Hyman Stahler
Sandra Fay Stahler

❧❀❧

Rabbi and Mrs. Moshe Stahler
Yaakov and Yosefa
Rabbi and Mrs. David Zharnest
Shira Chaya and Aharon Yehoshua

Dedicated in Cherished Memory of our

Dear Son and Brother

A loving heart and ben Torah

and a complete joy

to all who were priviledged to know him.

During his brief lifetime he brought us

only nachas and happiness.

The Feurman Family

כי אם בתורת ה' חפצו ובתורתו יהגה יומם ולילה

His desire is in the Torah of Hashem

and in his Torah he meditates day and night.

לזכר נשמות

מאלה בת ר׳ מרדכי יוסף

מישל בת ר׳ יצחק

גיטל בת ר׳ יצחק

אברהם יעקב ב״ר יצחק

Treblinka 1942

ר׳ יצחק ב״ר אברהם יעקב

ר׳ זאב ב״ר חיים צבי

יוטא בת ר׳ חיים יוסף

Mr. and Mrs. Abraham Feldstein and Family

❦

לזכר נשמת

אאמו״ר

ר׳ יוסף ב״ר שלמה הלוי ז״ל

שהלך לעולמו ביום ראשון לחודש מרחשון תשל״ב לפ״ק

ולזכר נשמת

מרת רבקה בת ר׳ ישראל הלוי ז״ל

שהלכה לעולמה ביום שני לחודש שבט תשל״ט לפ״ק

תנצב״ה

Rabbi and Mrs. Shlomo Wahrman and Family

In grateful appreciation to

the trustees and supporters of

The Susan Chesner Einbinder
Memorial Fund

whose continued support

has enabled many of our students

to enrich their lives with

the study of Torah.

May Hashem grant them

continued success in

all of their endeavors.

The

Hebrew Academy of West Queens

thanks all its

generous supporters

who have helped it grow

for the past twenty-six years

הסטוריה

The ArtScroll History Series®

Rabbi Nosson Scherman / Rabbi Meir Zlotowitz

General Editors

Published by

Mesorah Publications, ltd

GROWING UP IN NAZI LEIPZIG
1933-1939

by Rabbi Shlomo Wahrman

FIRST EDITION
First Impression . . . May, 1991

Published and Distributed by
MESORAH PUBLICATIONS, Ltd.
Brooklyn, New York 11232

Distributed in Israel by
MESORAH MAFITZIM / J. GROSSMAN
Rechov Harav Uziel 117
Jerusalem, Israel

Distributed in Australia & New Zealand by
GOLD'S BOOK & GIFT CO.
36 William Street
Balaclava 3183, Vic., Australia

Distributed in Europe by
J. LEHMANN HEBREW BOOKSELLERS
20 Cambridge Terrace
Gateshead, Tyne and Wear
England NE8 1RP

Distributed in South Africa by
KOLLEL BOOKSHOP
22 Muller Street
Yeoville 2198, South Africa

ARTSCROLL HISTORY SERIES ®
LEST WE FORGET
© *Copyright 1991, by* MESORAH PUBLICATIONS, Ltd.
4401 Second Avenue / Brooklyn, N.Y. 11232 / (718) 921-9000

ALL RIGHTS RESERVED.

*This text, prefatory and associated textual contents and introductions,
including the typographic layout, cover artwork, charts and maps
have been designed, edited and revised as to content, form and style.*

No part of this book may be reproduced
in any form *without* **written** *permission from the copyright holder,
except by a reviewer who wishes to quote brief passages in connection with a review
written for inclusion in magazines or newspapers.*

THE RIGHTS OF THE COPYRIGHT HOLDER WILL BE STRICTLY ENFORCED.

ISBN
0-89906-870-7 (hard cover)
0-89906-871-5 (paperback)

Typography by Compuscribe at ArtScroll Studios, Ltd.

Printed in the United States of America by Noble Book Press Corp.
Bound by Sefercraft, Quality Bookbinders, Ltd. Brooklyn, N.Y.

ספר זה מוקדש
לזכר נשמת
דודתי המהוללה והצנועה במעשיה

מרת **הינדא לאה** הי״ד בת ר׳ **ישראל הלוי** הי״ד

שנהרגה על קידוש השם
ע״י הנאצים הארורים ימ״ש

Dedicated
to the memory of my beloved aunt

Helene Kaufteil

Victim of the Nazi Holocaust

ארץ אל תכסי דמיה ואת דמם של כל הקדושים
שנהרגו על קידוש השם
עד אשר ישקיף ה׳ ממרום וינקום את דמיה
ויקבץ נדחי עמו ישראל בשמחה
לארצנו הקדושה והבנוי׳ במהרה בימינו

הסכמת

הרב הגאון מוהר״ר פנחס הירשפרונג שליט״א
ראש הרבנים במונטריאל

ב״ה

הנני בזה להגיד לאדם ישרו ה״ה הרב הגאון המפורסם חו״ב בכל
חדרי תורה מ׳ שלמה ווארמן שליט״א חובר חבורים מחוכמים וכבר
הדפיס חמשה חבורים אשר ראוהו גדולים ושבחוהו.

כעת חשקה נפשו להוציא לאור את זכרונותיו מימי המלחמה
ולהדפיס מה שעשו הנאצים ימ״ש לאחב״י, ואע״פ שכבר נדפס קצת
מה זה שעשה אותו העמלק ימ״ש. דבר זה מצוה מדאורייתא לקיים
זכור את אשר עשה לך עמלק – ובעל יון מצולה הדפיס ג״כ אודות זה
(על הגזירות הנוראות שנגזרו על היהודים בשנת ת״ח).

ולזאת חוב קדוש לספר למען ידעו הדורות הבאים את מעשה
התעתועים של הנאצים ימ״ש והעולם כולו ידעו מזה ולא עשו שום
מחאה.

הבה ונקוה כי הקב״ה ינקום את נקמתנו וישלם להנאצים שתהי׳ להם
מפלה במהרה דידן – אמן.

פנחס הירשפרונג

עש״ק פ׳ חיי שרה תשנ״א לפ״ק

מי יתן ראשי מים ועיני מקור דמעה ואבכה יומם ולילה את חללי בת
עמי (ירמיהו ח:כג).

ஃ Acknowledgments

I take this opportunity to express my most sincere appreciation to several people who helped make this work a reality.

When I approached my good friend, Rabbi Meir Zlotowitz, at the planning stages of this book and outlined its purpose to him, he immediately recognized its merits and encouraged me to commence with this project. Rabbi Nosson Scherman reviewed the original manuscript and offered many valuable suggestions. At all times I could count on his total cooperation, on his expert advice and guidance.

It is an honor, indeed, to be associated with men of such distinction, who through their many literary publications, are constantly spreading the word of genuine Torah among the masses. They are perhaps the greatest disseminators of *Hashem's* word today. I hereby extend to them my most sincere thanks and gratitude.

Rabbi Eli Kroen deserves special accolades with this volume. His efforts and artistic talents have made this volume a thing of real beauty. He follows the tradition of his mentor, Rabbi Sheah Brander, whose magnificent graphics skills have made the ArtScroll book respected and admired throughout the world.

Many of the ArtScroll-Mesorah Publications' staff have manifested their special skills and talents to produce this book. Among them, Rabbi Hillel Danziger, Rabbi Avie Gold, Mrs. Esther Feierstein, Bassie Goldstein, and Mrs. Tova Finkelman stand out. I would hereby like to express my deep appreciation to them and to the entire ArtScroll family who have contributed substantially, each in his own field of expertise. I am most grateful for their dedicated concern for exellence.

Mrs. Judi Dick's efforts should receive special mention. Her talents have immensely enhanced the quality of this book. Her penetrating questions and valuable suggestions were always on target. As a true friend, she worked beyond the call of duty and her enthusiasm for this project greatly inspired me. For all this, I am most grateful.

Mrs. Helen Frei spent many hours of her own time typing the original manuscript. Mrs. Debra Wenger meticulously reviewed the entire manuscript and immensely enhanced its quality. My own son Chaim Dov was in charge of all of the computer work prepared in our home.

I would, at this time, like to acknowledge the efforts of my wife in this project. As a survivor of the Auschwitz Concentration Camp, she is personally familiar with Nazi atrocities. Her constant encouragement certainly went a long way in motivating me to tell my story.

May *Hashem* grant that we derive much *nachas* from our children, Yaakov Elimelech and Faygie, Yisroel Shmuel and Miryam, Chaim Dov and from our grandchildren Shavie Shaindel and Shlomo, Miryam Chanah, Syma Esther, Yosef Yehudah Aryeh, Avigail Rivkah, and Shoshanah Nechomoh. May we merit the fulfillment of the *Navi's* prophecy, לֹא יָמוּשׁוּ מִפִּיךְ וּמִפִּי זַרְעֲךָ וּמִפִּי זֶרַע זַרְעֲךָ מֵעַתָּה וְעַד עוֹלָם (*Isaiah* 59:21) that in our family Torah will remain a way of life forever.

◆§ Contents

Lest We
Forget

Introduction

זָכוֹר אֵת אֲשֶׁר־עָשָׂה לְךָ עֲמָלֵק בַּדֶּרֶךְ בְּצֵאתְכֶם מִמִּצְרָיִם ...
לֹא תִּשְׁכָּח.

"Remember what Amalek did unto you on the way, as you came out of Egypt ... Do not forget it" (*Devarim* 25:17-19). This mandate is one of the 613 *mitzvos** of the Torah.

Many Biblical commentators have posed the question as to how we can fulfill this *mitzvah* today, when the identity of the present-day Amalek is unknown to us. Which nation is considered to be today's Amalekites?

The eminent *Gaon*, Rabbi Chaim Soloveichik of Brisk, teaches that the aforementioned *mitzvah* applies not only to the nation of Amalek, whom we are unable to identify today, but it applies equally to any nation which follows in Amalek's footsteps, any

---

* See Glossary for definitions of italicized terms.

nation for which cruelty and oppression against the Jews is a way of life.

Perhaps we can substantiate the Brisker *Rav's* view from the writings of Maimonides. When Maimonides discusses the laws pertaining to the seven Canaanite nations, he states emphatically, וּכְבָר אָבַד זִכְרָם, "their memory has already been eradicated" (*Hilchos Melachim* 5). Since Sennacherib intermingled the populations of the then-known nations of the world (*Berachos* 28a), we can no longer ascertain where the inhabitants of the seven nations are today. However, concerning the laws pertaining to Amalek, Maimonides makes no such statement. This would apparently bear out Rabbi Chaim's opinion that any nation which follows in Amalek's footsteps and plots to destroy the Jewish people is included in the *mitzvah* pertaining to Amalek. Undoubtedly, Hitler's Germany fits this description and is, therefore, a twentieth-century Amalek.

When Kaiser Wilhelm visited *Eretz Yisrael* in 1899, many of Jerusalem's residents went out to greet him. They were most anxious to recite the blessing of בָּרוּךְ . . . שֶׁנָתַן מִכְּבוֹדוֹ לְבָשָׂר וָדָם, *Blessed. . . Who has given of His glory to human beings*, which is recited upon seeing a king (*Berachos* 58a). However, the eminent *Gaon*, Rabbi Yosef Chaim Sonnenfeld, remained at home and did not participate in the official reception for the Kaiser, stating that no *brachah* is recited when seeing a king descended from Amalek. He quoted the opinion of the Vilna *Gaon* that Germany has the possible status of Amalek.

The *Yalkut Me'am Loez* states that when we read in the Passover *Haggadah*, שֶׁבְּכָל דוֹר וָדוֹר עוֹמְדִים עָלֵינוּ לְכַלוֹתֵנוּ, "in every generation they rise up against us to destroy us," we are referring to Amalek, who each time is embodied in a different nation. Thus, all enemies of the Jews are included in the *mitzvah* of remembering Amalek (*Devarim*, part 3).

אַל־תִּתֵּן ה' מַאֲוַיֵּי רָשָׁע זְמָמוֹ אַל־תָּפֵק. — "Grant not, O L-rd, the desires of the wicked; further not his evil device" (*Psalms* 140:4).

The Talmud states that this is a reference to "Germamya of Edom." אִלְמָלֵי הֵן יוֹצְאִין הָיוּ מַחֲרִיבִין כָּל הָעוֹלָם כּוּלוֹ, "If they were permitted to roam freely, they would destroy the entire world" (*Megillah* 6b). Amalek is a descendant of Edom (*Bereishis* 36). More than two centuries ago, the renowned scholar, Rabbi Yaakov Emden, stated in his commentary of the Talmud that this Talmudic text is a reference to Germany. One can easily note the striking resemblance between the name Germany and the "Germamya" mentioned in the Talmud. Thus, the *mitzvah* of *Zachor* (Remember) applies to Germany today.

This *mitzvah* of *Zachor*, then, was the motivation for writing this book. As early as the 1950's, HaGaon Rabbi Eliezer Silver had urged me to recount my personal experiences in the Nazi inferno, in compliance with the *mitzvah* of remembering the evil deeds of the Amalekites. It is my solemn duty to publish a book on the subject, he apprised me.

I later questioned HaGaon Rabbi Moshe Feinstein as to the necessity of writing such a book, in light of the fact that so many books on the Holocaust had already been published. What would be the purpose of yet another work?

Rabbi Feinstein felt that the world requires constant reminders of the tragic events of the Nazi era, especially when we see contemporary anti-Semitic groups investing so much effort to prove that the Holocaust never happened. Books depicting the Holocaust are usually read, placed on the bookshelf, and then forgotten. Rabbi Feinstein assured me that any additional book would arouse a renewed interest in the subject. I, too, would be revealing new facts which had not yet come to light. Thus, my obligation under the mitzvah of *Zachor* was quite clear.

I was born in Leipzig, a town which is situated in the northwestern corner of the East German province of Saxony. When our family immigrated to the United States in 1939, I was merely a young lad of twelve. During those twelve years I had witnessed Leipzig Jewry reach its peak population of 18,000 in

1935, and in the four ensuing years, I saw it dwindle to 6,000. Eventually Leipzig was to become totally *Judenrein*.

In the summer of 1980, I returned to my home town. Even though World War II had ended thirty-five years earlier, the results of the Allied bombings were still clearly visible in this Communist stronghold. I recognized the narrow streets and alleys, many of which had been completely obliterated by the Allied air forces, and I recognized the now-dilapidated buildings which comprised the old Jewish neighborhood in the vicinity of the *Hauptbahnhof*. Physically, at least, the city was still recognizable.

However, the city was now devoid of any Jewish content. Its Jewish inhabitants had been barbarously massacred, and only 54 Jews still remained there. (When I returned again in 1990, the number had dwindled to a mere 36.) Jewish organizations and community facilities had vanished. Only the Broder Shul, the cemeteries, and several memorial plaques scattered around town remained. They served as the lone reminders of a once-flourishing community.

Although I had expected to be confronted with these prevailing conditions, I was, nevertheless, heartbroken. I shed many tears during my two-day visit to my home town as I compared the Leipzig which had existed in the 1930's with the Leipzig which greeted me in 1980. I realized that the Leipzig of my youth could no longer be located on a Jewish map. It had simply ceased to exist. A total spiritual *churban* was now manifest throughout the city. Here in Leipzig, my sister sadly observed, Hitler — *yemach shemo* — had achieved complete success. For all practical purposes, Leipzig had indeed become *Judenrein*.

As I perused the indices of many Holocaust publications, I rarely found any reference to the city of Leipzig, which was my home. The destruction of the Jewish Leipzig, much to my disappointment, was related only sporadically in these books. I then became convinced that the story of the *churban* of Jewish Leipzig, a city where *Yiddishkeit* had abounded and blossomed for so many years, must be told. It must be preserved for all future generations.

This work is not intended to be a documentary of the events of the Nazi period. It is, rather, a narrative composed of personal experiences during those dark days. It should be noted that the events related here were those I witnessed and participated in as a youngster under the age of twelve, and they are recorded now, some fifty-one years later, without the benefit of any diary or memorandum. To supplement these memoirs and to place events into proper perspective, I have relied on some excellent documentary histories published on the Holocaust.

In 1915, the Turks drove the majority of the people of Armenia out into the wastes of the desert. Hundreds of thousands of Armenians died of starvation, exhaustion, and sunstroke in the desert. Experts estimate that more than a million additional Armenians perished during World War I. However, this massacre was soon forgotten by the world. When Hitler's advisers cautioned him that the world would not stand idly by as the Jews were being annihilated, he replied, "Who still speaks today of the massacre of the Armenians?" The genocide against the Jews, he felt, would just as quickly be forgotten.

I hope that this publication will help to arouse awareness of the Holocaust among us and aid in the continued study of its implications. Public outrage and revulsion at the Holocaust is a most potent weapon in preventing its recurrence. The world must never be permitted to forget what it did.

One

Jewish Community of Leipzig
Before the Holocaust

EIPZIG LIES IN EAST CENTRAL GERMANY, in the northwestern corner of the province of Saxony. Its location at the junction of the Elster, Pleisse and Parthe Rivers makes it a major port. A canal connects Leipzig with the Elbe and Saale Rivers.

The city of Leipzig was chartered in 1174. Because it lay at the intersection of several European trade routes, it grew rapidly into a **The City of Leipzig** trading center. It later became world famous for its trade fairs and gained a reputation as one of the greatest literary and musical centers of Europe.

There are many schools, art galleries, and museums in Leipzig. The University of Leipzig was founded in 1409. One of its most

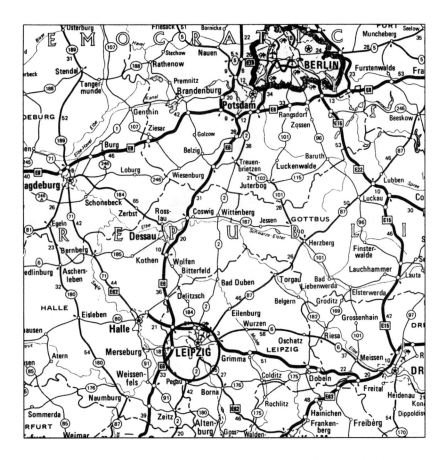

famous graduates was the great German poet, Johann Wolfgang von Goethe. Other Leipzig schools included a conservatory founded by the composer Felix Mendelssohn in 1843, an art college, and an academy of graphic and literary arts.

Leipzig has played a prominent role in the history of German music. Johann Sebastian Bach, Robert Schumann, Felix Mendelssohn, and other musical figures lived in the city. The composer Richard Wagner and the philosopher Gottfried Leibniz were born there.

The city first became a battleground during the religious wars of the 1600's. The first battle of Leipzig was fought near the city in 1631. In this battle, Swedish forces, led by Gustavus Adolphus,

Leipzig's Voelkerschlacht Denkmal, a monument commemorating the battles for the city

won a great victory over the German army. The second Battle of Leipzig, fought between the Germans and Swedes in 1642, also resulted in a victory for the Swedish forces, who then continued to occupy the city for several years. In 1813, in the third Battle of Leipzig, Napoleon was soundly defeated by the forces of Prussia, Russia, Austria and Sweden.

During World War II, Allied forces occupied the city. After the war, the Soviets took over Leipzig and revived the *Leipziger Messe*, its two great industrial fairs, which occured in the spring and fall.

JEWS ARE FIRST MENTIONED IN THE HISTORY OF LEIPZIG at the end of the twelfth century. An organized Jewish community,

The Jewish Community of Leipzig with a synagogue and religious school, existed as early as the second quarter of the thirteenth century. Its inhabitants came mainly from the neighboring towns of Halle and Merseburg.

The renowned Talmudist of the early thirteenth century, Rabbi Yitzchok ben Moshe of Vienna, mentions the community and its synagogue in a responsum in his classic *sefer, Or Zaru'a.* The responsum discusses a Jew who came to Leipzig for the purpose of collecting some business debts on behalf of his father, and turned to the community's religious court to render a halachic decision on a dispute which ensued in this matter.

Although the *Messe* (Fair) regulations of Leipzig guaranteed equal protection to all merchants, and the market day was moved from Saturday to Friday for the benefit of the Jewish merchants, there is ample evidence that Leipzig's Jews suffered greatly during the Black Death persecutions of 1348-1350, and that their numbers dwindled. As a result, in 1352, the *Markgraf* of Meissen disposed of the Schule der Juden in Leipzig. The building, which had served both as a synagogue and as a religious school, was awarded to one of the *Markgraf's* feudal lords.

In 1359, we hear of a *Judengasse* near the city's wall, and in 1364, a *Schulmeister* and other Jews are mentioned. These Jews lived in the *Judenburg*, which had its own entrance gate.

The Jews of Leipzig were probably not expelled in 1442 as the city historians record, though their status surely deteriorated, but were banished from Leipzig only after the expulsion of the Jews from all of Saxony in 1540. However, their right to attend the fairs, which were then held three times a year, remained unaltered. Between 1668 and 1764, more than 80,000 Jews attended the *Leipziger Messe*, and the Jewish participation decisively influenced the success of these fairs. Leipzig's growth as the center of the fur trade was largely due to Jewish activities. The wealthiest Polish merchant once arrived at the *Messe* with forty wagons filled with furs, and many of Leipzig's merchants were his business partners. The steady stream of *Messe* visitors reached such huge proportions that it became imperative to operate special kitchens for them. In 1756, no less than 140 workers were employed to operate these kitchens in an orderly, effective fashion.

Stores facing the Hinterhaus, crowded alleys rather than streets

In 1769, the *Kurfuerst* appointed a Jew to prepare and supervise all activities of his fellow Jews who would visit the *Messe*. By the end of the eighteenth century, six Jewish families had been appointed to perform these tasks. These Jews came to be known as *Schutzjuden,* and they were permitted permanent residence in the city.

Jews, however, were prohibited from opening shops facing the streets. Even as late as the 1930's, one could still see many places of business facing the *Hinterhaus*, yards, and crowded alleys. This was especially true of the Bruehl, the Reichsstrasse, and other neighboring areas of the city.

The Bruehl was the temporary home of so many Jewish merchants who visited Leipzig for the *Messe* that it came to be known as the *Leipziger Judenstat*. In 1763, a *shtibel* was organized by visiting Galician Jews. The *shtibel* was called the *Broder Betstube*, since many of the visiting Jews originated in Brody, which, at that time, was the center of trade in northern Galicia. This *shtibel* was the forerunner of the large Broder Synagogue, which still stands today on the Keilstrasse.

In 1727, in his constant search for additional sources of funds, the *Kurfuerst* August made it mandatory for Jewish fair visitors to obtain a *kammerpaesse* to permit them the privilege of entering Leipzig. Wealthy Jewish merchants gladly paid the required fee for this passport, because presentation of it often spared them from troublesome and embarrassing inconveniences usually directed at Jews and helped cut much of the red tape. Jews at that time were also required to pay *schutzgeld* to the local authorities.

A permanent Jewish settlement was established in Leipzig during the eighteenth century, and by the end of that century, forty to fifty Jewish merchants were living in the city. These merchants employed clerks, servants, agents, and *shochtim*.

By the year 1835 there were as many as seven *shtiblach* in Leipzig, all organized and directed by *Messe* visitors from Poland and Galicia. At the same time, the number of permanent Jewish residents increased rapidly. Even when, in 1837, a law was issued in Saxony officially permitting the establishment of an organized Jewish community, permission to build a synagogue was withheld. However, a prayer house, influenced by Reform tendencies, was opened at that time. Eventually, permission was granted to construct a synagogue, and in 1855, the new synagogue in the centrally located Gottschedstrasse was dedicated.

It should be noted at this time that since the overwhelming majority of Leipzig's permanent Jewish residents were of the

Reform persuasion, the synagogue, later to become known as the *Gemeindesynagogue* or simply the "Tempel," certainly did not conduct its religious services in compliance with Orthodox standards. Therefore, the small number of Jewish residents at the time who conducted their lives strictly according to *halachah*, and who refused to budge even an iota from the *Shulchan Aruch*, found it virtually impossible to participate in religious services at the "Tempel."

After 1868-69, with the abolition of all anti-Jewish restrictions, the number of Jews was augmented greatly by immigration from Poland and Galicia. These newcomers were generally referred to as *Ostjuden* by the Jews of German origin. There were 4,294 Jews living in Leipzig in 1890; 6,171 in 1900; 7,676 in 1905; and by 1925 the Jewish population had risen to 13,032, making it the largest Jewish community in Saxony.

Religious Life in the Early Twentieth Century

SATISFYING THE RELIGIOUS REQUIREMENTS of such a vast multitude of immigrating *Ostjuden* who were mainly Torah-observing Orthodox Jews mandated the undertaking of new initiatives. As a result, the *Talmud Torah Verein* was organized in 1900, and its immediate task was to construct an Orthodox synagogue. The chairman of this new *Verein* was Herr Joseph Binyamin Sacks.

Due mainly to the philanthropic endeavors of the Kroch family, who generously contributed most of the needed funds, construction of the new sanctuary commenced the following year. Thus, in 1904, the Broder Shul was dedicated. This magnificent edifice, situated on the Keilstrasse in the heartland of the Orthodox community, incorporated the many *shtiblach* that existed at that time. The Broder Shul, or as many referred to it, the Kroch Shul, soon became the center of Orthodox Jewish life in Leipzig. From

The Broder Shul

within its walls emanated many new ideas and initiatives so vital to the continued growth of a vibrant Jewish community.

The Broder Shul complied fully with all regulations of *halachah*. Women prayed in an upstairs gallery which surrounded three sides of the sanctuary. The *bimah* was situated at the center of the *shul*, as prescribed by rabbinic authorities. The spiritual leader was the renowned scholar, Rabbi Ephraim Carlebach, who had received his rabbinical training in the Hildesheimer Yeshivah in Berlin. Rabbi Carlebach was appointed to this position in 1901 by the newly-founded *Talmud Torah Verein*, which was an independent organization and, therefore, like the Broder Shul itself, was not under the auspices of the *Religionsgemeinde*. It should be pointed out, however, that in regard to non-religious matters pertaining to Jewry as a whole, Rabbi Carlebach worked in complete harmony with the *Religionsgemeinde*.

Hillel Schneider served as cantor of the *shul*, and remained in this position until Kristallnacht, by which time he had already reached his late seventies. Before the anti-*shechitah* laws went into effect in Germany, Schneider was also a *shochet* par excellence, reliable and trusted by all. In addition, Cantor Schneider served as a *mohel* for many boys born to Orthodox families. He was a kind and gentle man, possessing an unusually warm personality; he

Rabbi Ephraim Carlebach

was extremely pious, admired and respected by all. His face was adorned by a long, flowing white beard, which added dignity to his persona.

As the Orthodox community continued to grow and prosper by leaps and bounds, it became necessary to establish additional *shuls* and *shtiblach*. Many houses of prayer were organized by various *Landsmannschaften*. These *shuls* were founded by Eastern European Jews and named after the members' birthplaces or Eastern European residences. The Yasser, the Bochner, the Krakauer, the Lemberger, and the Kolomeaer Shuls all belonged to this category. A *shtibel* was also established on the Leibnizstrasse by the renowned Chassidic *Rebbe* Rabbi Friedman, a member of the Boyaner Chassidic dynasty which has followers in many communities throughout the world.

September 10, 1922 marked an historic day in Leipzig's Orthodox Jewish annals. On that day, the Eitz Chaim Synagogue on the Otto-Schill Strasse (Apels Garten) was dedicated. The construction of this beautiful edifice, which became the largest Orthodox synagogue in Leipzig by far, was made possible due to the generous contribution of the philanthropic Eitingon family. Chaim Eitingon was an *Ostjude* who had arrived in Leipzig from

Prayer room at the Religionsgemeinde

Sklow, Russia, at the end of the nineteenth century. He became a successful businessman in the fur market, and eventually became known as the Koenig vom Bruehl. Rabbi Carlebach was immediately appointed as the spiritual leader of the new synagogue, and thus both the Broder Shul and the Eitz Chaim became his responsibility. Although his base of operations was generally the Otto-Schill Strasse, he would often attend services at the Keilstrasse. He would usually officiate at the latter on the second day of all major holidays. When a decision on *halachah* had to be rendered during Rabbi Carlebach's absence, the venerable Rabbi Auerbach, who was then in his late eighties, was consulted.

The Eitz Chaim Synagogue engaged the world-renowned cantor, Chazzan Nochum Wilkomirsky, who eventually directed an all-male choir to assist him during services. The *shul* was usually filled to capacity when Wilkomirsky officiated. Even people who preferred to pray in other *shuls* would, upon completion of their own services, come to the Otto-Schill Strasse just to hear Wilkomirsky lead the congregation during *Mussaf*.

Experts on liturgical music — and Leipzig had many — considered him to be second to none. He favorably compared to the likes of such giants as Rosenblatt and Kwartin. What a *chazzan* he was!

EDUCATION ALWAYS PLAYS A PROMINENT ROLE in the makeup of any Jewish community. Torah education is the

Jewish Education in Leipzig

backbone which insures Judaism's continued existence in future generations. Therefore, in 1912, Rabbi Carlebach went to work on this project and the Hoehere Israelitische Schule came into being. In 1913, the new school building on the Gustav Adolf Strasse was dedicated. Rabbi Carlebach had labored feverishly and spared no effort in achieving this cherished goal; it was for this

The Hoehere Israelitische Schule

reason that many began to refer to the newly-founded school as the Carlebach Schule.

In 1927, the Ahavath Torah Synagogue on the Faerberstrasse opened an afternoon religious school to supplement the education that the youngsters received at the Carlebach Schule. Rabbi David Feldman became the spiritual director of this new Talmud Torah, and due mainly to his great talents and self-sacrificing devotion, the Talmud Torah rose to lofty heights.

Rabbi Feldman was held in great esteem by his congregants. He was a renowned Talmudic scholar, whose *Metzudas Dovid* commentary on the *Kitzur Shulchan Aruch* has become a classic and has been reprinted numerous times. In the early 1930's, he emigrated to England, where he became the spiritual leader of the Kehillah Machzikey Hadas in Manchester, England. Rabbi Feldman's warm and cheerful personality could melt even the iciest heart. His concern for the welfare and felicity of each and every one of his students knew no bounds. Thus, he was able to wield great influence over the students and guide them in the proper path.

The curriculum of the Carlebach Schule consisted of both religious and secular subjects. The religious courses taught were Bible, Prophets, and Jewish history; in addition, *Mishnayos* and Talmud were taught in the upper grades. Rabbi Carlebach himself was the Talmud instructor in the highest grade, and his reputation of being a phenomenal *rebbi* was widespread.

As only eight hours were allotted to religious studies each week, one could not really receive a well-rounded Jewish education at the Carlebach Schule. Certainly the school could not produce the genuine *talmidei chachomim* who are so necessary for the guidance of future generations. Therefore, the Faerberstrasse Talmud Torah became a vital ingredient in Leipzig's religious educational system.

The name "Talmud Torah" which Rabbi Feldman chose for his school was a misnomer, and it was certainly misleading. The

קצור

שלחן ערוך

עם

כללים נחוצים

מכתב־יד שלא נדפס עדיין

מאת הגאון המחבר ר' שלמה גאנצפריד ז'ל

עם

עיר דוד

המכיל

מצודת ציון / מצודת דוד / המתרגם / שער הציורים

שיעורי המצוות / לוח הקביעות / נוסח שטרות ועוד

כמבואר בהקדמה

מאתי

דוד פעלדמאן בלאמו'ר הרב ר' שמאי ז'ל

שלפנים רב דקהל' יראים בלייפצינג (אשכנז)

וכעת אב'ד רסחזיקי הדת בסנשסהר יע'א

תוצאה חמישית

מנשסתר   תשי"א   ניו־יורק

Title page of the Kitzur Shulchan Aruch
with Rabbi David Feldman's commentary, Ir David

school was actually a small yeshivah, whose standards and quality of education compared favorably with many of the *yeshivos ketanos* existing in the United States today.

The Talmud Torah's curriculum was quite ambitious. Classes would commence at 4 p.m. each weekday and at 9 a.m. on Sunday mornings. The school offered twelve hours of religious instruction weekly. Nine of those hours were devoted exclusively to *Mishnah* and *Gemara*, one hour for laws and customs, and two for the weekly Torah portion with *Rashi's* commentary.

A child would generally begin his Talmudic training at the age of nine and a half, and by the time he reached the age of *Bar Mitzvah*, he would have absorbed more than one hundred *blatt* of *Gemara*. Monthly examinations were conducted under the keen supervision of Rabbi Feldman and Rabbi Eliyahu Moshe Rogosnitzky (who replaced Rabbi Feldman when the latter emigrated to Manchester) to assure that each youngster was progressing in his studies and that he was on his way to becoming a genuine *lamdan* and *ben Torah*.

All of us were extremely fond of our *rebbeim* in the Talmud Torah, even though corporal punishment was very much in style at the time. Generally, when a student was chastised and disciplined by the *rebbi*, he made every effort to conceal these proceedings from his parents. The parents almost always sided with the *rebbi* (and they were usually right).

After *Bar Mitzvah*, the boys were adequately prepared to continue their studies at a more advanced level in institutions of higher learning. Some continued in the Yeshivah Rabbi Solomon Breuer in Frankfurt am Main; some travelled all the way to the Mirrer Yeshivah in Poland; but the overwhelming majority made their way to the Yeshivah Eitz Chaim in Heide, a suburb of Antwerp, Belgium.

Unfortunately, not all students were privileged to avail themselves of the Talmud Torah program. Some had been raised in irreligious homes and their parents were quite satisfied with the religious education offered at the Carlebach Schule. At that school, a youngster became familiar with his own ethnic background and culture and with the history of his people. The school succeeded in instilling within the children a love of Torah and a love of Judaism. This, these parents felt, was quite sufficient for their children's needs.

Registering their children in a German Christian school was out of the question and was not even contemplated by these parents. Can a youngster become imbued with such intense feelings for Judaism, with a love and sense of pride in his people, while attending a Christian school, where anti-Semitism reigned even before the advent of the Hitler era? Yet, even up to the uncertain 1930's, there were some Leipzig Jews, though not many, who were so thoroughly permeated with the principles of liberalism and equality that they were prepared to tolerate abuse and degradation for the sake of these principles. To display their solidarity with the German masses, these Jews registered their children in Christian schools, although they knew quite well that they were unwanted by the masses.

That their efforts should end in failure and tragedy was inevitable. Often we witnessed their children returning from school, which they were obligated to attend even on *Shabbos* with foul-mouthed harassing Nazi youths following close behind, heaping insult upon insult on their Jewish victims. Usually these offensive indignities were followed by physical violence and blood was spilled. It was surely a most pathetic sight. I vividly remember one occasion in which a Jewish child had to be rushed to a doctor for emergency care as a result of this harassment.

I felt it was happening to them because they went to school where they were not wanted. The fact that Christians harassed Jews really didn't shock me. I was used to that and I was not really afraid; just resigned.

Despite the constant harassment and physical attacks by Nazi hoodlums, the life of a Jewish youngster in Leipzig was a pleasant one. Since we resided in a strictly Orthodox section of town, we had much in common with our friends. We wore our "Jewish" brown caps publicly with pride and shared in the resulting explosive consequences. We attended the same school and the same Talmud Torah. Above all, we stuck together as a group and that armed us with the courage, fortitude, and stamina so necessary to adapt in hostile surroundings.

Intolerance was the very cement which shaped Leipzig's schools even before the Hitler era. Dr. Fleissner, the Minister of Culture for the province of Saxony, issued an edict mandating Jewish students to attend classes on *Shabbos* and other Jewish holidays and to participate in all class activities, including writing, drawing, and needlework. Although this edict was eventually withdrawn for the Jewish High Holidays, it nevertheless remained in effect for *Shabbos* and other holidays. In one celebrated case, when Dr. Felix Goldmann took his son to shul on *Shabbos* instead of allowing him to attend classes, he was fined twenty-five marks. His appeal to a higher court was unsuccessful.

Jewish education was not confined merely to the classroom. Each *Shabbos* afternoon, youth groups would meet, under the sponsorship of the Mizrachi organization, in the Elsterstrasse *Jugendhaus* for an *Oneg Shabbos*. Other groups would meet at the Talmud Torah on the Faerberstrasse under the auspices of the Agudath Israel youth movement known as Ezra. Although these sessions certainly could not be construed to be formal learning classes, nevertheless a world of learning took place there. The refreshments served helped to create a more serene and tranquil atmosphere, which proved to be a marvelous stimulant to learning.

Herr Potok, a *rebbi* at the Talmud Torah, would often visit these sessions. Despite the fact that his German was colored by a heavy Yiddish accent and was, at times, difficult to understand, the stories he related were always both fascinating and entertaining. Each story contained an inspirational message. These stories taught us to appreciate and to treasure the greatness and the eminence of our distinguished *gedolim* of past generations. We learned of the appropriate character traits that a true *ben Torah* should possess, and we learned how to live a life saturated by Torah and *mitzvos*.

Herr Potok was surely a most fascinating individual who displayed a sincere love for every child. I am still not quite sure why he insisted that we address him as Herr Potok, rather than Rabbi Potok. We were all aware of the fact that he had received his *semichah* from the leading Torah authorities of Poland.

Herr Potok, by far, was my favorite and most influential *rebbi*. He was able to instill within me a love for Torah and a genuine desire for learning. While preparing to immigrate to the United States, I often expressed my concern, "Where in the U.S. will I find another *rebbi* like Herr Potok?" A *rebbi* of his caliber is rare, indeed.

Leipzig was surely a city abounding in the study of Torah. Torah was in the very air one breathed. Each synagogue offered *shiurim* on various topics for people at all different levels of learning. Here one could always find a *shiur* in Talmud, studied in depth at a very advanced level. At the same time, classes were available in the study of *Mishnayos*, Bible and Prophets. There were even classes for beginners whose background in Torah was extremely shallow. The opportunities were available for all.

One could walk into the Ahavath Torah Synagogue at Faerberstrasse 11, or into the Chevrah Mishnayos Shul on Humboldtstrasse 24 (a shul generally known simply as the "Vierundzwanzig" [24]) at any time of the day and discover a *shul* packed with adults studying Torah. The Tifereth Yehuda Synagogue (the Bernstein Shul) at Eberhardstrasse 11 was always filled with men learning and discussing various intricate passages in the Talmud.

IT WAS NOT SURPRISING THAT LEIPZIG was the home of so many distinguished Torah scholars who earned their livelihood in

Leipzig's Torah Personalities

the business world. The Kroch family was one of the wealthiest families in Germany. They were the owners of Leipzig's "Hoch-haus," a ten-story structure on the Augustus-platz in the city's center. From there they conducted their extensive business affairs, dealing mainly with stocks and bonds. Their firm was also known as the giant in the grain market.

The family's philanthropic activities for all Jewish causes were

Hochhaus on the Augustus Platz. It was owned by the philanthropic Kroch Family

well known to Leipzig Jewry. The construction of the Broder Shul served as a graphic model of their widespread charitable endeavors.

Yaakov Leib Kroch, the father of these wealthy businessmen, would dedicate many hours of his day to the study of Torah. Eventually he became an erudite scholar and authored many books. Although nothing was published during his lifetime, the mass of writing which he left behind was eventually published by his grandson Pinchas Yaakov as an eleven-volume work entitled *Chazakah Rabbah*. The last volume of this opus, as well as three volumes of *Halachah Rabbah*, were later published in Jerusalem. In these books, Reb Yaakov Leib dealt capably with a most intricate halachic concept, one with ramifications throughout all the volumes of the Talmud. Immediately upon publication, these *seforim* received commendations from leading Torah authorities, who hailed his work as an outstanding achievement in the Torah world.

Reb Leib Merkin was a simple and ordinary businessman who earned his livelihood in the fur market on Leipzig's Bruehl. He was a warm individual who had a kind greeting and a pleasant comment for all who came in contact with him. He was a genuine *ohev Yisrael*. Yet at the same time, Reb Leib was a *talmid chacham* of the highest caliber. His numerous business obligations never deterred him from his most cherished aspiration, that of expanding upon his already vast knowledge of Torah and of improving his comprehension of its concepts. "One must continue to grow both spiritually and academically," he once remarked to my father. That, succinctly, was his goal in life.

Once, when I was about six, my mother sent me to Rabbi Feldman with a *shailah*. He was to make a halachic decision pertaining to the *kashrus* status of a chicken. When I arrived at the Feldman residence, I found the rabbi deeply engaged in a heated debate with Reb Leib regarding an accurate interpretation of a certain Talmudic text. *Seforim* had been piled high on the table,

חזקה רבה

מיוסד על כללי חזקות דאיסורא ודממונא· שרשם פתוח עלי מים נאמנים·
ים התלמוד ופוסקים ראשונים ואחרונים· אשר היו לנו למאורות,
ילקוט אבנים יקרות· סברות ישרות· פנים מסבירות· להבין ולהורות·
ולתרץ קושיות חמורות· יצהירו בין השורות· אשר העלה ואשר הביא·
תני וכייל בכיילא רבה· איש חמודות· התמים בדעות· יבין שמועות·
מברר ומלבן סוגיות עמוקות והלכות גדולות· זקן שקנה חכמה ודעת·
הרב החריף ובקי בכל חדרי תורה· כל רז לא אניס ליה·

מוה"ר יעקב ליב קראך זצ"ל

סדרו והוציאו לאור
פנחס יעקב הכהן

חלק שני (א)
על
יורה דעה

ליפסיא
שנת ספר חזקה רבה יו"ד א' (תרפ"ח) לפ"ק

CHASAKAH RABBAH
LEIPZIG
1928

Title page of Rabbi Yaakov Leib Kroch's work, Chazakah Rabbah

Jewish Community of Leipzig before the Holocaust / 37

with each participant attempting to prove the accuracy of his own contention. The debate was conducted at such a feverish pace, and the two gentlemen were so involved in their discussion, that more than an hour passed before the rabbi even noticed my presence in the room. After offering a most courteous apology to me, then but a lad of six, the rabbi, with Reb Leib's approval, proceeded to *pasken* the *shailah*.

When I later reported this incident to my father, he unhesitatingly informed me that Reb Leib's erudition in areas of Torah ranked favorably with that of the leading Torah authorities. Of course, Rabbi Feldman treated him as an intellectual equal. Herr Potok added that very few people were really able to appreciate Reb Leib's *gadlus*.

Rav Shmuel Halpern, a Galician-born scholar who received his rabbinic ordination from the renowned Torah giant the *Maharsham* (Rav Sholom Mordechai of Berezhany), was one of the early leaders of Leipzig's Orthodox community. He settled in Leipzig right after the conclusion of World War I and successfully organized the Kehillah Machzikey Hadas. Due to his outstanding scholarship and majestic personality, his influence was felt far and wide. His valiant efforts on behalf of Orthodoxy bore fruit. They certainly went a long way in making Leipzig the Torah community it was.

However, Rav Halpern remained in Leipzig for only several years. Eventually he settled in Israel and became the spiritual leader of Agudath Israel in Tel Aviv. When his younger brother, Rav Yaakov, later organized the new *shechunah* of Zichron Meir in B'nei Brak, he was installed as the neighborhood's first rabbi.

A few brief words concerning the lofty stature of Rabbi Rogosnitzky, the Rabbi of the Ohel Yaakov Synagogue, would certainly be in order here as well. This great *gaon* of Lithuanian descent was the product of the *yeshivos* of Lithuania. In April 1938, he authored a brilliant halachic commentary which contained some profound thoughts and poignant observations, and

Rabbi Shmuel Halpern

mailed it to the renowned Rabbi Reuven Katz, the chief rabbi of Petach Tikvah, Israel. Rabbi Katz's response appears in his sefer *Degel Reuven*. He marveled at Rabbi Rogosnitzky's patience and strength of character in being able to concentrate on academic Torah issues at a time when he and his countrymen were suffering from such ferocious and cruel attacks.

Rabbi Rogosnitzky was a gracious and most affable individual, whose hospitality knew no bounds. There were always out-of-town guests boarding in his home. The rabbi would generously offer tea and cake to all those who came to ask a *shailah*. In those days, it must be remembered, telephones were practically nonexistent, so that *shailos* had to be asked in person.

To the children, especially, Rabbi Rogosnitzky displayed a genuine and unbounded love. He never failed to inquire about their progress in Torah and in his soft Lithuanian Yiddish, he was able to motivate many youngsters to attain greater diligence in their studies.

I last saw Rabbi Rogosnitzky on a *Shabbos* several weeks after Kristallnacht. I was greatly appalled when I noticed that most of his beard had been cut by the Nazis. "How low they have sunk," I thought to myself. "How can any human abuse a man so devout and so pious?" Now, fifty-two years later, I still shudder whenever the picture of the rabbi and his shortened beard enters my mind. I still remember him embracing me after *Shabbos* services and bestowing his blessing upon me. "You have the potential of becoming a great *lamdan*," he told me. I have never forgotten his kind words of encouragement. He was certainly a great man.

These and many other such intellectual giants, such as Rabbis Schmuckler and Melamed, helped turn Leipzig's Orthodox section into an authentic Jewish neighborhood where *Yiddishkeit* filled the air. But, alas, the pain is great when one realizes, or especially when one witnesses in person, that none of this still exists today. The Jews have disappeared (only 36 remain) and this once fertile land has been turned into a barren wilderness.

My Family in Leipzig

MY PARENTS WERE BORN AND RAISED IN GALICIA, which became an integral part of Poland upon the conclusion of World War I. My father was descended from a lineage studded with such eminent *gedolim* as Harav Avraham Dovid Wahrman of Butchach who authored the classic *sefer Da'as Kedoshim* and Harav Shlomo Kluger, the *maggid* of Brody. My father's ancestry could be traced directly all the way back to King David.

My parents were raised in traditional homes, where the Chassidic way of life dominated. For generations, their ancestors had been dedicated followers and adherents of the renowned Chassidic dynasty, the *Rebbeim* of Belz.

After World War I, when anti-Semitism was on the constant rise in many European countries, countless poverty-stricken Jews emigrated from Galicia in pursuit of a better life. My own parents immigrated to Germany in either 1925 or 1926, for the German Weimar Republic offered many new economic opportunities. They settled in Leipzig, where the overwhelming majority of Orthodox Jews originated from Galicia.

Yiddish, with a heavy Galician dialect, was the predominant language in our home during my pre-school days. Only upon entering the first grade at the Carlebach Schule did I actually begin to converse in German.

My parents settled in Leipzig's city center whose inhabitants were mainly *Ostjuden*. Although Hinda Kaufteil, my mother's sister, and Liba Seid, my grandmother's sister, were our only relatives residing in Leipzig, my parents were able to adjust beautifully to their new surroundings. They felt quite at home among so many Galician Jews — some even originating from their own home towns, Zaloscie and Szcrzorowice, both in the vicinity of Brody. However, the overwhelming majority of our relatives continued to reside in Galicia.

Though both of my parents were born in Poland, their Polish citizenship was eventually revoked by the Polish regime and their new nationality was listed as *statenlos* (stateless).

Despite their valiant efforts to obtain a Polish visa which would enable them to visit their parents and other close relatives who resided in Poland, their efforts were not crowned with success. A visa was never granted. As a result, my father never saw his mother after 1925 and my mother never again saw her father. My maternal grandmother did come to visit us in Leipzig three times, whenever my mother gave birth. I can still recall seeing her in 1928, when my sister Rachel was born, and again in 1932, when my brother Shimon was born.

Even at present, I can still visualize my grandmother, leaning against a warm oven, reciting chapters from the Book of Psalms and reading from the classic *sefer Tz'enah Ur'enah*. Often she would sing to me Yiddish songs describing our Patriarchs, our Matriarchs, and the twelve sons of Yaakov.

My father, like so many of our neighbors, at first earned his livelihood as a travelling salesman of silverware. Eventually, however, together with my Aunt Hinda, he became the proprietor of a silverware store on the Nordstrasse. He was also active as one of the community's *shochtim*.

To supplement this income, we would rent out rooms in our apartment to industry representatives from various European countries, who came to attend Leipzig's *Messe* twice a year. It was during such times that the entire family would have to crowd into the remaining rooms.

My family was very close-knit. There was a mutual feeling of love between each of us. We were content with our lot in life. As youngsters, we never realized our financial woes. As far as we were concerned, we were rich. We possessed everything we ever needed. Didn't our Sages teach: אֵיזֶהוּ עָשִׁיר הַשָּׂמֵחַ בְּחֶלְקוֹ, *Who is a wealthy person: One who is happy with his lot.*

The families of my closest friends, Reuven Bieder (who now resides in the U.S.) and Gerhard Goldfaden (who to the best of my knowledge was deported to a concentration camp), like so many of Leipzig's Jewish families, were in the same financial bracket as we were. They could afford only the bare necessities of life. So instead of money, we had friendship and love. We had each other.

I resided in Leipzig for the first twelve years of my life and in this short period, we resided at five different locations. The first residence was on the Gottschedstrasse. We shared the apartment with another family and when my sister was born, we were forced to move to larger quarters.

So we moved to the Reichstrasse in the heart of the Jewish fur district. My parents were never quite happy on the Reichstrasse. Although the house was in close proximity to the Tiktiner Shul and the Eitz Chaim Shul on the Otto Schill Strasse and all apartments in the house were occupied by Orthodox Jewish families, it was nevertheless not an ideal place to live in. The constant foul odors which emanated from the many fur establishments in the yard made living there quite unpleasant, especially during the hot summer nights. In addition, our apartment was located in the *Hinterhaus* where no windows faced the street. So my parents began searching for a new apartment.

The fact that I was rapidly approaching school age and the Reichstrasse was a long way from the Carlebach Schule, hastened their search. Eventually we moved to the Eberhardstrasse which was within easy walking distance from the *Schule*. It was an ideal location. The Bernstein Shul was right across the street and the Broder Shul only two short blocks away. The Nordstrasse, right around the corner, offered the best Jewish shopping in all of Leipzig.

In 1935 or 1936, we rented an apartment on the Nordstrasse because it was contiguous to a store and we would have our business right next to our home. This was probably our only residence in Leipzig which would not be considered a slum by American standards. The apartment was bright and spacious. We even had a tiny garden in the back of the house.

Approximately six weeks before we emigrated from Leipzig, we relinquished the apartment. The authorities required a huge monetary deposit from all Jews to cover all possible expenses should the Jews decide to leave the country without prior notification of the authorities. So we moved to the Faerberstrasse where the Brenner family rented us one large room. There we remained until our departure.

Not many of Leipzig's *Ostjuden* lived a life of wealth and affluence. Many families barely eked out a living. Yet, Leipzig's Orthodox Jews were a close-knit community, with a sense of duty and responsibility. Each one appeared to care and was ready to pitch in when the situation so required. It was a happy community.

My own family was always content with their station in life. My parents' major concern was whether I was progressing in my studies. When I began the study of the Talmud before I reached the age of nine, my mother was so proud that soon every one of our neighbors was aware of my accomplishment. I remember my father proudly writing his mother in Poland informing her of my progress.

Despite suffering persecutions at the hands of Nazi hoodlums, our life in Leipzig was generally a happy one. Unfortunately, it ended too soon.

THE YEAR 1924 MARKED A DRAMATIC CHANGE in the composition of Leipzig's *Gemeinde*. Following a long period of discussion,

The Last Years of Jewish Leipzig when all opposing views had been fully aired, the Orthodox community officially joined the *Gemeinde* and Rabbi Carlebach became *Gemeinde Rabbiner*. Israel Stein and J. B. Sacks became the Orthodox representatives to the *Gemeinde's* Board of Directors. Orthodox Jews would now actively participate in *Gemeinde* functions, they would share its burdens, and they would reap the benefits accorded to its entire membership.

Although the Orthodox rabbinate was to retain total autonomy in all matters pertaining to religion, opposition to this union never faded away. According to my father, it continued well into the Hitler era. However, during my most recent visit to Leipzig in July 1990, when the *Gemeinde's* membership books were at my disposal, I meticulously searched for many names of residents who, in my estimation, would have opposed the union. I found all their names recorded in the membership books. Perhaps in the 1930's, all recognized the importance of maintaining a united Jewish front opposing the Nazi authorities and thus, all opposition finally abated.

In 1925, the *Gemeindeblatt* began its weekly publication, and it soon became the mouthpiece of Leipzig's Jewry. It reported scrupulously all community activities, and its editorials served to motivate Jews to constantly strive for progress and proficiency, and to encourage them when catastrophe appeared imminent. It often helped lighten the burden of impending tragedy in those troubled times by publishing a more optimistic scenario of forthcoming events, one filled with hope and prospects for salvation.

Although the *Gemeindeblatt* adhered faithfully to the halachic rule of *deena d'malchusa deena*, which mandated the Jews to faithfully observe the government's laws as free and patriotic German citizens, it often spoke out courageously and steadfastly whenever it felt that Jewish rights had been violated. The paper

Juden Leipzigs - Männer - Frauen - Deutsche - Ausländer

Eure Pflicht ist am 6. Dezember nur

die vereinigte orthodoxe Liste 4 Stein - Schumer - Weigler

Goldmann, Dr. Nobel, Dr. Dzialowski zu wählen.

Unser Programm: Fürsorge für alle religiösen und sozialen Bedürfnisse der Gemeinde.

Wählt die einzige orthodoxe Liste 4 Stein - Dr. Dzialowski

Orthodox campaign literature during the 1925 elections
for representatives to the Religionsgemeinde

thus became the champion of Jewish rights.

The *Gemeindeblatt* continued its uninterrupted publication until November 4, 1938, just several days before Kristallnacht. On November 8, 1938, the government ominously forbade publication of Jewish newspapers, thus outlawing three major newspapers, the *Central Vereins Zeitung*, with a circulation of 40,000 copies; the *Juedische Rundschau*, circulation 26,000; and the *Israelitisches Wochenblatt*, circulation 25,000. In addition, the government closed down four cultural periodicals, sports magazines, and twenty-five community bulletins, including Leipzig's *Gemeindeblatt*. The Berlin bulletin alone had a circulation of 40,000. In this way, the government eliminated a major source of information and communication available to the Jews and increased their isolation.

It is most interesting to note that while in November 1933 a total of 4,500 copies of the *Gemeindeblatt* were printed, as clearly indicated at the top of the newspaper, by May 1936 this number had been cut down to 3,600. The reason is obvious. The Jewish population in Leipzig had reached its peak in the years 1933-35, when there were more than 18,000 Jews residing there. When the Nazi regime came into power and introduced its anti-Semitic decrees, Jewish emigration commenced gradually. With the introduction of the infamous Nuremberg laws in 1935,* emigra-

---

* An in-depth description of these laws is found in Chapter Three.

Bannerheads of Leipzig's Gemeindeblatt. Note the decrease in circulation of 4,500 in November, 1933, to 3,600, in May,1936

tion continued at a more rapid pace, and by 1936 it was in full swing. Thus, with the dwindling of the Jewish population, the circulation of the *Gemeindeblatt* was drastically cut.

1936 was also the year in which my own family came to the realization that we could not survive in Germany for much longer. My father eventually wrote to his sister in New York, asking her to send us the necessary affidavit so that we, too, could immigrate to the United States.

Leipzig's Jewry was fortunate in one respect. Whenever the need for a new project arose, kindhearted individuals stepped to the forefront to donate the necessary funds. When the community felt the vital need for a Jewish hospital, there was the ever-ready Eitingon family, most anxious to assume all financial responsibili-

Chaim Eitingon

Alexandra Eitingon

ties for this costly undertaking. "Chaim and Alexandra Eitingon are Leipzig's very own Montefiore," was the appropriate comment of the *Gemeindeblatt*.

In 1928, *Das Juedische Krankenhaus* opened its doors, the first Jewish hospital in the province of Saxony. It was a magnificent structure with all modern and up-to-date facilities. The Eitingon family had purchased the most expensive medical equipment

The Jewish (Eitingon) Hospital

Jewish Community of Leipzig before the Holocaust / 47

available at the time, and medical authorities hailed it as one of the best and most fully-equipped hospitals of its time.

Today, the hospital still stands. It is still considered top-notch. But with only 36 elderly Jews remaining in Leipzig, many no longer residing in the area, its facilities are hardly ever used by Jewish patients. Of course, the kosher kitchen no longer exists. It is, therefore, difficult for me to still refer to it as the "Jewish Hospital." What's Jewish about it?

Since I remain firmly convinced that most of Leipzig's Christian inhabitants were, and many still are, ardent anti-Semites (I have spoken to enough Germans in recent years to be able to draw this conclusion), many of those very same anti-Semites, who were actively persecuting Jews during the Holocaust, undoubtedly are utilizing the "Jewish" hospital's facilities today. I have often wondered about the feelings of these anti- Semites as they are being treated and healed in a hospital founded by Jews, the same Jews they once referred to as the *verfluchte Juden*. Is there at least a tinge of regret?

The Communist regime which governed Leipzig from 1945, in a gesture of friendship and appreciation, named the hospital street the Eitingonstrasse. Thus, they showed recognition to this family and to their philanthropic accomplishments. Their name will forever be enshrined within the city of Leipzig. What a sad reminder of the Jewish Leipzig which once existed and prospered, in which the Eitingons played such a prominent role! Surely they never envisioned being honored in a "city without Jews," whose inhabitants participated in the murder of six million of their fellow Jews.

In 1931, *Das Juedische Altersheim* was opened on the Auenstrasse. It was a most generous gift presented to the elderly with love and affection by the noble Frau Louise Ariowitsch and dedicated to the memory of her late husband, Max. The home contained everything that the life of a pious and devout Jew required. There was a beautiful synagogue on the ground floor.

The Ariowitsch Home for the Elderly

There were three separate kitchens — for dairy, for meat, and for Pesach — furnished with modern appliances. All rules of hygiene were staunchly and resolutely adhered to. Everything possible was done to enhance the comfort and convenience of the elderly residents.

Yes, Leipzig was surely a community with heart. It steadfastly concerned itself with the welfare of the poor and underprivileged. Many social action programs were available. There was a public kitchen to feed the hungry; there was a free loan association which offered assistance to those temporarily in need; there was an organization whose function was to find work for the unemployed; and there were many other organizations to serve the needs of the helpless and downtrodden.

Thus, Jews were able to reside in Leipzig as Jews, among friends, in a serene and tranquil atmosphere. Leipzig Jews thanked *Hashem* for their lot in life. There was a feeling of contentment and peace of mind. Little did anyone even consider the possibility that all of this "heaven on earth" would soon vanish. Not in his wildest dreams could anyone imagine that in just a few short years, the community would be totally destroyed and that "Jewish Leipzig" would be wiped off the map, never to appear again.

Chapter Two

A Child in Leipzig in the 1930's

 WAS A YOUNGSTER IN THE FIRST GRADE OF SCHOOL in 1933, when President Paul Hindenburg appointed Adolf Hitler to serve as Chancellor of Germany. I have no recollection whatsoever of this tragic day. My earliest memory of any significant political event in Germany was Hindenburg's demise in August 1934. In observance

My Father the Shochet of his death, all stores were closed on the day of his funeral. Upon Hindenburg's death, Hitler assumed full power and became the absolute dictator of Germany.

Of course, being a mere child, I had no inkling of the

significance of this new order. Since I had no knowledge of Hitler's violent and anti-Semitic background, I did not entertain even the vaguest notion that this would somehow affect the future of all European Jewry. As far as I was concerned, life continued as usual.

A short time after Hindenburg's appointment of Hitler, an announcement appeared in the *Gemeindeblatt* that on the following *Shabbos*, Rabbi David Feldman would be addressing Leipzig's Jews in the Broder Shul; he would be discussing a topic of major significance. On the following *Shabbos*, at the designated hour, the Broder Shul was filled to the rafters.

Rabbi Feldman discussed with us the legislation of April 21, 1933, which effectively banned *shechitah* (ritual slaughter) in Germany. Since through the process of legal technicalities and loopholes employed by the Nazi regime the importation of kosher meat from foreign countries was virtually impossible, Rabbi Feldman announced that kosher meat would no longer be available in Leipzig at all.

The law of *shechitah* is of Biblical origin. It has been suggested that the Jewish method of slaughter, particularly the laws that the knife be exceedingly sharp and without the slightest imperfection, were motivated by consideration for the animal, because this method is most painless. Laws and other indications in the Bible make it quite clear that not only is cruelty to animals forbidden, but also that compassion and mercy to them is demanded of man. *Tza'ar ba'alei chaim,,* concern for the pain of living creatures, plays a significant role in the Jewish religion. The *shechitah* procedure was thus devised to make animal slaughter instantaneous and painless. Maimonides, in his "Guide to the Perplexed," writes in a similar vein: "Since the desire to procure good food necessitates the slaying of animals, the law enjoins that the death of the animal should be as easy and painless as possible."

Despite this, there have been occasional attempts in the non-Jewish world to ban *shechitah*. While some of these were motivated by humanitarian concerns, in many cases the agitation was merely a manifestation of anti-Semitism.

Many of the opponents of *shechitah* have advocated electrical stunning of the animal before the act of *shechitah*, which would render the animal unconscious and thus insensitive to pain. However, the renowned *Gaon* Rabbi Chaim Ozer Grodzensky of Vilna and many other Torah luminaries have emphatically declared that the *halachah* strongly opposes such stunning. Stunning often causes a strong jerk of the muscles which could impair the act of *shechitah*. It may also injure the animal's brain and lungs, rendering the animal forbidden. The stunning, furthermore, causes extravasation of blood so that small blood clots form in the meat; causes hemorrhages; and causes severe congestion of muscles. These problems are discussed in detail in the classic *S'ridei Eish* by Rabbi J. Weinberg, who headed the Hildesheimer Yeshivah in Berlin.

When I expressed a sense of concern and annoyance at these latest developments, my father related that during World War I, when his family was forced to flee from Galicia, they were able to subsist on nothing but potatoes for weeks at a time. With *Hashem's* help, he assured me, we would survive without meat.

Much to my astonishment, I soon discovered that in spite of the ban on *shechitah*, we continued to eat chicken at regular intervals. I was quite puzzled by this development. If *shechitah* was forbidden, why were these chickens permitted? Didn't the law of *shechitah* apply equally to all animals? When I presented this conundrum to my parents, I was not granted a satisfactory answer despite my obstinacy and persistence in repeating the question. I was simply told that I was too young to understand this.

Eventually, I discovered the answer to my question. A small group of courageous *shochtim* was performing the act of *shechitah* on chickens in a secret and surreptitious manner, which fortunately had gone undetected by the Nazi authorities. Thousands of chickens were thus being slaughtered each week for the consumption of Leipzig's religious community. I soon discovered that my own father was one of these *shochtim*. One could well imagine the reaction of the Nazi regime had they discovered and apprehended these *shochtim* and formally charged them with this gross violation of their ban. Fortunately, however, this never came to pass during our years in Leipzig.

One could only marvel at the solidarity displayed by Leipzig's Jewish community at that time. Hundreds, perhaps even thousands, of Jews were fully aware of who the *shochtim* were. In my own class of more than thirty students, everyone was familiar with the fact that my father was illegally slaughtering chickens. The authorities constantly dispatched inspectors to all Jewish chicken markets searching for violators. Informers would most certainly have made a favorable impression on the Nazis. Perhaps they would even have been compensated for their cooperation. And yet, no Jew took the bait. No Jew sank to the depths of informing on his fellow Jews, and no violators were ever discovered. What a marvelous demonstration of Jewish unity!

It would, at this point, be fitting and proper to list the names of these courageous individuals who defied the Hitler regime on behalf of keeping *kashrus*. Unfortunately, however, Schwarzbart, Tykoschinski, Printz, and Hendler are the only names I am able to recall.

During the days immediately following Kristallnacht, when "stateless" Jews were rounded up to be dispatched to the Buchenwald concentration camp, a Gestapo agent arrived at the Hendler home searching for Herr Hendler. Though he was not at home at the time, the message to him was quite clear. He wasted no time making his way to the *Hauptbahnhof*, and soon found himself on a train heading for the Belgian border. Although *Shochet* Hendler did not possess a Belgian visa, he was nevertheless able to enter Belgian territory. A small number of border guards had been bribed to assist Jews in their efforts to reach the safety of

Belgium in their flight from persecution, and these guards lived up to their part of the bargain. In this way, more than 150 Leipzig families made their way to Antwerp to what turned out to be only a temporary respite. In June 1940, the German Wehrmacht conquered Belgium, and these hapless Jews found themselves under the Nazi boot once again.

By the end of 1938, all the other *shochtim* had emigrated from Germany, so my father remained Leipzig's sole practicing *shochet*. He remained faithfully at his post until our family's departure from Leipzig on April 11, 1939.

We have heard reports that upon our departure another gentleman consented to fill my father's dangerous position. Though leading Polish rabbis had granted this man *kabbalah* for *shechitah* as early as the 1920's, he had up to this point never practiced it; he had earned his livelihood as a merchant. Now, due to this exigency, he succumbed to the pressure applied by community leaders and responded positively to their pleas. A short time thereafter, according to these reports, a Gestapo agent arrested him while he was in the act of performing his sacred task, and he was never heard from again.

My father's hazardous occupation created much anguish for my mother, especially when we discovered that a gentile neighbor was familiar with my father's activities. My mother lived in a state of constant fear. Her face changed color each time my father left the house. My father, of course, took every precaution and kept an extremely low profile. Often, my younger sister would carry the *chalef* (*shechitah* knife) to the chicken market because we were confident that the Gestapo would not apprehend such a young girl. Nonetheless, my mother remained tense. Even when we were in Hamburg, preparing to board the S.S. Roosevelt which would bring us to the United States, she was still apprehensive and kept reminding us that we were still in Germany; we were still not out of the reach of the Gestapo.

As a youngster, I did not share my mother's anguish at first.

However, I do remember one particular day when this message came through to me loud and clear.

While opening a chicken, my mother discovered a defective liver and was thus uncertain about the *kashrus* of this particular bird. Since I happened to be available at the time, she asked me to go to Rabbi Rogosnitzky to ascertain the chicken's status — was it kosher or *treif?*

On the way to see the rabbi, I discovered that a uniformed SS officer was walking right behind me. I was suddenly gripped by a deathly fear. I was convinced beyond any shadow of doubt that I was being followed. It was bad enough being trailed by the SS, but here I was carrying contraband and I felt my pulse racing as the fear coursed through my body.

Questions began to crowd my mind. Why was the SS officer following me? What if the officer asked me about the paper bag I was carrying? Should I tell him that I was heading for the rabbi's home? Why was I going to see the rabbi? Could I mention *kashrus*, when for all practical purposes kosher meat was not supposed to be available anymore? Would I be the one who would blow the cover off the entire Jewish *kashrus* operation? I was seized with trepidation, as I knew that the SS had always been portrayed as the most barbaric and anti-Semitic of all the Nazi groups.

Fortunately, the SS officer turned out not to be at all interested in me, and my internal alarm was for naught. I was greatly relieved. I felt as if a heavy burden had been lifted from my shoulders. But having undergone several minutes of severe panic, I now realized for the first time the perilous time in which we lived, and the danger that enveloped us all. Perhaps, then, my mother's anguish was indeed justified.

Despite the *shechitah* ban and the widely publicized prohibition of the rabbinate, one Leipzig butcher continued to conduct business as usual with whatever meat he could procure, and did not even see fit to remove the "kosher" signs from his premises. Most Jews, though, even including some who had never observed *kashrus* before, refused to purchase any meat at this establishment. Consuming this meat, it was felt, would be showing compliance with Hitler's wishes to place *treif* food on every Jewish table. In our opposition to Hitler, everyone stuck together.

Occasionally we received packages of kosher delicatessen from our relatives in Poland. Since German law prohibited receiving food packages from other countries unless the recipient was on welfare, our relatives had to mail these packages to a Jewish family who was on welfare, and our two families then shared their contents.

WHEN THE NAZI REGIME CAME TO POWER IN 1933, the aim of their policy vis-a-vis the Jews was to make Germany *Judenrein*. By **The** making life unbearable for the Jews, the **Anti-Jewish** Germans would force them to emigrate. Nazi **Boycott** policy was to use all possible means to eliminate Jews from the German state and society, assigning the racial principle as the dominant guide for the Third Reich. The Jews were thus eliminated from citizenship, public office, the professions, and the intellectual and artistic life of the country. Public schools were barred to Jewish children on November 15, 1938.

On April 10, 1933 an anti-Jewish boycott was initiated throughout Germany. SS officers were stationed in front of Jewish stores, urging Germans not to purchase from the Jews. Each Jewish store on Leipzig's Bruehl was effectively blocked by the SS, who permitted no one to enter. This boycott was accompanied by fierce anti-Jewish propaganda from the ministry of Josef Goebbels, and with minor incidents of violence against individual Jews.

The impression abroad concerning the boycott was decidedly unfavorable. A counter-boycott movement was begun against German exports and was supported by Jews and non-Jews alike. This boycott reached a point at which Reichsbank Praesident Hjalmar Schacht pointed out that the unlawful activities against

An anti-Jewish
boycott poster,
telling Germans
not to patronize
Jewish
businesses

the Jews would have to end; otherwise, he, Schacht, would not be able to cope with his task of economic rearmament.

To give a few examples, Schacht reported the activities of boycott chief Streicher, who was attempting to force German firms to dismiss their Jewish representatives in foreign countries. Schacht, however, also noted that these Jewish representatives were "especially skillful." When the Jewish agent of Alliance Insurance in Egypt was subjected to party chicanery, he simply quit and took his business with him. In many cities, including Leipzig, Jews were not permitted in public baths. How was that going to work out during the Leipziger *Messe*, when so many foreign businessmen, many of them Jews, attended the fair?

Furthermore, continued Schacht, this unlawful activity had provoked a counter-action abroad. Outside importers were boycotting German firms as a reaction to the boycott of Jews. A French importer had canceled a large order he had placed with Salamander Shoes. The Bosch firm had lost its entire South American market. These were only two examples of the adverse results of the boycott.

Schacht stated that whoever maintained that one could do without the Jewish business simply did not understand the business world. Jews were needed even for importing, because the trade in rare products, which were needed by the armed forces, was in Jewish hands.

This did not mean, Schacht concluded, that all single actions against Jews were to be condemned. He could see no objection to the display of signs reading *"Juden unerwuenscht"* (Jews not wanted).

Germany's Interior Minister, Frick, fully agreed with Schacht that wild single actions against Jews would have to stop. The "Jewish question" would have to be handled in a perfectly legal manner.

The policies of Streicher's vicious newspaper *Der Stuermer* were sharply rebuked by Schacht. The director of a local Reichsbank office, one of Schacht's own men, had bought something from a Jew who had served as a sergeant in World War I and had received the Iron Cross. Thereupon, Streicher displayed a picture of the *Reichsbankrat* on three public bulletin boards, and under the picture he captioned, "Whoever buys from a Jew is a traitor to the people."

Schacht replied with indignation that as a non-party member, this director had every right to buy wherever he pleased. He knew of no law to the contrary. He reiterated that he opposed "wild" party measures. He preferred the legal way. In 1935, even Streicher finally declared that the Jewish problem was being solved "piece by piece" in a legal manner. New laws and decrees were in the process of being prepared.

Headlines from Streicher's "Der Steurmer" exclaim:
"The Jews are our misfortune! — Death to the desecrators of the race."

It should be pointed out that German Jews generally opposed an anti-German boycott by the rest of the world. They were convinced that not only would it not help to improve their lot, but that in fact it might prove to be counterproductive. Furthermore, they felt that if the boycott succeeded in weakening the German economy, it would be an equal blow to the Jews since they, too, would suffer as a result. In an editorial, the Berlin-based *Juedische Rundschau* made a fervent appeal to worldwide Jewry to desist from any boycott measures.

Once the Nazis gained full power, it did not take very long for signs to be posted in all non-Jewish stores in Leipzig, along with all other cities and towns, declaring that Jews were not welcome in their establishments: *"Juden unerwuenscht."* Often, this was followed by the Stuermer's Jew-baiting slogan, *"Die Juden sind unser Unglueck"* (the Jews are our misfortune).

Sign proclaims: "Jews not welcome here."

Strict adherence to these signs by the merchants and businessmen could potentially make the Jews' predicament critical. In many cases Jews would be denied access to the very necessities of life. Over the doors of grocery stores, bakeries, and dairies the signs proclaimed clearly for all to see that Jews were not admitted. Pharmacies would not sell them medicines. Hotels would not give them a night's lodging. Always, wherever the Jews went now, were the taunting signs, "Jews strictly forbidden in this town" or "Jews enter this place at their own risk."

Although the consensus was unanimous in considering these signs to be extremely degrading, and they succeeded in their intended purpose of downgrading the self-esteem of the Jewish people, surprisingly no one panicked. A crisis atmosphere was not created. All types of merchandise were still readily available in the many shops owned by Jews. "This is not the end of the world," many stated. "With the help of *Hashem*, we will manage."

Unfortunately, however, there was no Jewish pharmacy in our section of town. The closest pharmacy was on the Gerberstrasse, and its proprietor had in the past been an outspoken critic of anything even vaguely connected to Judaism.

I was probably nine or ten years old when my parents sent me to that pharmacy to fill a doctor's prescription. I reluctantly consented to go. Since I was well aware of the pharmacist's negative opinion of Jews I was not expecting a picnic, and in this feeling the owner did not disappoint me.

As I entered the store, my greeting of *guten Tag* was answered with a resounding "Heil Hitler!" This had become the newest German greeting, which was used in all occasions. I suddenly found myself in a most degrading and humiliating situation. My sense of pride and self-respect had disintegrated. The man had explicitly stated that I was not welcome there, and here I was forcing myself upon him.

I decided to wait my turn, but it did not come quickly. The pharmacist ignored my presence completely. Customers who entered the store much later than I did, even other boys my age, were served before me. I simply kept waiting. I did not protest my mistreatment for fear of creating an incident. Finally, when no other customers remained in the store, the pharmacist turned to me with a harsh "What do you want?" I gave him the prescription and he filled it, but when he handed me the medicine he suggested that perhaps, in the future, I could take my business to another pharmacy. I did not reply. My *auf Wiedersehen* upon my departure was again answered with a rousing "Heil Hitler!"

When I left the store I was depressed and dejected, greatly concerned about the fate of my fellow Jews. But then I began to reflect about what I had just experienced, and the more I contemplated the situation, the more I realized that I was dealing with a lowly creature who possessed not one iota of humanity, one who would discriminate against a young boy solely because he was not a member of his so-called "master race." At that moment I offered my thanks to *Hashem* for having been born to Jewish parents who were raising me to a life of Torah, whose ways are ways of pleasantness and all of its paths are paths of peace. Despite my sorry plight, I was both overjoyed and proud to be a Jew at that moment.

DURING THE EARLY NAZI YEARS, the subject of brown caps became a controversial issue among some of Leipzig's Jews.

Trouble for the Children Leipzig's students of all schools wore specially designed caps. The caps for all schools were alike in design; only their colors differed. The color of the Carlebach Schule caps was brown.

Some Jews felt that by wearing these caps, children were publicly identifying themselves as Jews, something which would only serve to incur the wrath of the German masses. These well-intentioned people strongly advocated the old policy of "be a Jew at home and a German on the street." *Ostjuden*, many of whom wore beards, and whose dress differed substantially from that of the average German, were specifically targeted. Why must Jews be so conspicuous in public and present such a high profile? These were the people whose mentors, earlier in the century, had vehemently opposed the very founding of the Carlebach Schule for fear that it would create a self-imposed ghetto within Leipzig and would eventually ignite the flames of anti-Semitism.

Rabbi David Ochs, a graduate of the Hildesheimer Yeshivah in Berlin, who became the Orthodox *Gemeinderabbiner* in 1936

Class at the Talmud Torah. Note several students wearing the shielded brown cap.

when Rabbi Carlebach emigrated to Palestine, defended the brown cap. "Concealing one's Jewish identity," he declared, "will not save us. The anti-Semites know who we are and they will find us even if we abandon the brown cap. Jews must take pride in their religion and as long as they are within the confines of the law, nothing should compel them to modify their mode of dress or alter any of their customs."

Rabbi David Ochs

Although many new decrees were constantly being issued by the German government, life for Jewish youngsters did not change drastically. We were subject to the same type of attacks from the early 1930's up to the Kristallnacht period. These attacks were usually initiated by the *Hitler Jugend* with name-calling and insults. *Verfluchter Jude* and *Schmutziger Jude* were standards. We simply ignored these taunts and did not respond. Often, we would cross the street or head for another street in our effort to avoid them. We did everything possible not to create an incident which could have wide repercussions.

But our efforts were not always crowned with success. The thugs followed us. Occasionally these encounters would culminate with fisticuffs. They always outnumbered us and we were usually on the losing side. Several times I returned home with a cut chin or a bloody nose or lip. Once my finger was broken by one of Hitler's hoodlums. We were so accustomed to this that we took it for granted. We made nothing of it.

I can recall only one occasion in which it appeared that we got the better of the altercation. After an encounter with German youths, we noticed some blood on my friend's shirt. (I can no longer remember this friend's name.) Since none of us was bleeding at the time, we naturally concluded that the blood was that of one of the Nazi youths, who had apparently been injured during the encounter. A feeling of satisfaction and a sense of victory overcame all of us. For once we had been able to teach the Nazis a well-deserved lesson. We had given them some of their own medicine.

However, my friend's face suddenly turned pale, and soon he was sobbing uncontrollably. "How could I have done such a thing?" he kept repeating to himself. "How could I have spilled human blood?"

Our response was that we had certainly acted in self-defense and it was thus permissible. This did not alleviate my friend's feeling of guilt, however. He insisted, *"Ich habe menschliches Blut vergrossen"* (I have spilled human blood). All our attempts to placate him and to justify his actions proved to be futile and fell on deaf ears.

When this incident was later reported to our *rebbi*, Herr Potok, he was reminded of the saying of our Sages that Jews are *rachmonim*, people who are merciful toward others (*Yevamos* 79a). He commented that it seemed that Jews display mercy even toward their professed enemies, even toward those who attack them physically. To be merciful to others is certainly an innate Jewish trait. It is the very guiding principle of the Jews.

Generally, however, our frequent encounters with the *Hitler Jugend* were much more painful and physically damaging. After a while, though, we became accustomed to them and the hurt seemed to diminish. Even the humiliating trips to the pharmacy became less so after the first several times, when I became inured to the taunts and insults hurled at me.

Physical abuse soon escalated to outright robbery at the hands of Hitler's youth movement. Usually, a group of five to ten of these hoodlums, all possessing "master race" credentials, would accost individual Jewish children on their way to school, hurt them physically, and conclude the assaults by forcibly appropriating their briefcases. All of this was carried out in an atmosphere of hilarity and high-spirited boisterousness, to further humiliate and degrade the innocent victims. The all-too-familiar *verfluchter Jude* and *raus von Deutschland* slogans usually featured prominently in these proceedings.

Often the contents of these briefcases would be discovered several days later. They were usually found scattered in an abandoned area, often in the mud or in a puddle of water. This outrage became so common and widespread that it was experienced by most of my classmates at one time or another. We generally accepted it as a way of life in Nazi Germany. It was something over which we had no control. What could we do?

When my own briefcase was forcibly seized by Hitler's thugs, my father decided to report this matter to the police. Unfortunately, however, the police sergeant displayed little interest in our complaint. He dismissed it as a simple children's prank with no racial overtones, and informed us that he was much too busy to be bothered with such nonsense.

The sergeant quickly changed the subject. He inquired as to whether I had been treading upon the beautiful lawns of the Rosenthal, a park in our immediate area. When I replied that I had not, a thorough cross-examination ensued. Had any of my Jewish friends been trampling these lawns? Are they the ones who are guilty of destroying the beautiful scenery in the Rosenthal? Again my reply was in the negative. At this last response, the sergeant's anger really exploded.

"Someone has been doing it, and we're going to catch the culprit!" he roared. "Tell that to your Jewish friends!" he screamed hysterically.

I was obviously quite shaken by these insinuations and by the harshness with which they were presented, since I knew that the charges were totally groundless. Never had I witnessed any of my "Jewish friends" violating any of the Rosenthal's regulations. We had always been quite meticulous in observing the law. As a matter of fact, I had often observed Christians, both children and adults, trampling on those very same lawns, in full view of the police, and creating havoc in the park. So why was this innuendo cast upon the character and reputation of Jewish youngsters? The sergeant's diatribe merely served to confirm once again, if any confirmation was still necessary at this point, the prejudicial hostility and animosity of the Germans toward the Jews.

So much for justice for the Jews in Leipzig, my father commented to me sadly as we left the police station. (My briefcase, incidentally, was never recovered.)

❀ ❀ ❀

The less-than-cooperative attitude of the police can also be shown in the following incident, which also illustrates the fact that Leipzig's Jews, even in the early years of the Hitler regime, lived in a state of fear and apprehension, often bordering on hysteria.

In October 1935, my brother Shimon, only three years old at the time, left the house to walk across the street to watch my father construct the *succah* in the yard of Eberhardtstrasse 11. When, approximately an hour later, my mother went down to bring him lunch, she discovered that he had never arrived in the *sukkah* area. My father had not seen him all morning. He had simply disappeared.

A sudden feeling of alarm and panic gripped my mother. She began to weep uncontrollably. Being fully aware of the Jews' plight in German society and the Germans' lack of any compassion toward our people, my mother was convinced beyond a shadow of a doubt that my brother had been abducted by Nazi hoodlums. This seemed to be the sentiment of many of our friends, although at the time none of them shared their feelings with my parents. On the contrary, only optimistic words of comfort were expressed to my parents. They were assured that my brother would be found.

Immediately, a frantic search for my brother was initiated. Twenty to thirty of our friends and neighbors searched each and every house and apartment within the immediate and surrounding areas. We notified the police. No stone was left unturned. But it was to no avail. No trace of my brother could be found.

About three hours later, a policeman, making his usual rounds and realizing that a child had disappeared in our neighborhood, informed us that an unidentified boy had been found wandering aimlessly at the *Hauptbahnhof* and was at present in police custody. My parents rushed to the station, where they found my brother calmly chewing on an apple and wondering about all the commotion. Needless to say, it was a most joyful reunion.

None of the members of the search party for my brother had gone to the *Hauptbahnhof*, even though it was merely a ten-minute walk from our house. To reach the *Hauptbahnhof*, one had to cross the Bluecherstrasse (now Rudolf

The Hauptbahnhof, located in Leipzig's Jewish Section

Brietscheid Strasse), and everyone reasoned that such a small child could not possibly cross that traffic-congested street safely.

However, my brother had been in police custody for almost two hours. Since we had notified the police of his disappearance, we wondered why the police had not contacted us earlier. A police officer assured us that there was absolutely no anti-Semitism involved. The delay was due solely to the poor communication systems between the various departments of the police. Despite gut reactions to the contrary, my parents had no choice but to accept this explanation.

❈ ❈ ❈

Bad Duerrenberg was a health spa in the vicinity of Leipzig where many Germans spent their summer vacations. It was there that the Jewish *Gemeinde* sponsored a summer camp for children. Since the camp was too small to accept all applicants, the policy

The summer-home for children at Bad Duerrenberg

was to accept youngsters on a first-come, first-served basis. Thus, the camp was always filled to capacity.

However, in one particular summer, either in 1933 or 1934, many children returned home several days after their arrival in camp. It seems that the structure facing the camp's main building had been plastered with huge signs and posters declaring, *Die Juden sind unser Unglueck* and *Tod den Juedischen Rassen-schaendern* (the Jews are our misfortune and death to the Jewish desecrators of our race). Since up to that time no such posters had appeared in Leipzig on a regular basis, the Bad Duerrenberg signs really alarmed the parents, who considered them to be the kind of provocation which could foster a full-scale pogrom in this small town.

I can still recall quite vividly a brief period of great panic and terror we once experienced during my vacation stay in the Bad Duerrenberg camp, probably in 1935. A large group of forty to fifty Nazi thugs had gathered in front of the main camp building, and they were shouting racist and anti-Semitic slogans. *"Juden, raus von Bad Duerrenberg!"* (Jews, get out of Bad Duerrenberg!) they screamed boisterously. It was their obvious intent to make Bad Duerrenberg *Judenrein.*

Inside the building, we felt that we were under siege. We were convinced that the Nazis would break into the camp grounds at any moment and create total havoc. Personally, I expected a pogrom. Fortunately, however, the camp director was able to notify the police, who arrived quickly and dispersed the rowdy demonstrators. To the best of my knowledge, they never returned to the camp area. They had already made their point.

But the thirty minutes we had spent in a state of terror affected many of the young campers emotionally. Some were too fearful and apprehensive to leave the camp premises for the rest of the trip. It was not much of a vacation for them.

In the years that followed, though, the camp was again filled with children. People had become accustomed to these anti-Semitic slogans and demonstrations as a mark of everyday life, and they disregarded them. They were no longer cause for alarm or panic.

❧ ❧ ❧

Despite the constant tension in the air, the Jewish holidays were especially happy occasions for us. The streets of our neighborhood, the paths of the nearby Rosenthal, were packed with friends on a leisurely stroll, all dressed in their *Yom Tov* finery. I can recall several occasions when a large group of my classmates would inadvertently meet in the Rosenthal. We would proceed to occupy several benches, and sing holiday melodies. This was done in full view of Christian onlookers who generally mocked and taunted us during these sessions. But who paid any attention to them? It was our *Yom Tov* and we were going to enjoy every moment of it.

Three

The Exodus Begins

LL THROUGH THE EARLY 1930'S, anti-Semitic outbursts continued unabated. This brought many Jews to the realization that Germany was no longer safe for them as a home. Some emigration began, but the majority of the Jews remained. Large-scale emigration did not begin until the end of 1935, when the notorious Nuremberg Laws were passed. Then it became virtually unanimous. Emigration was the only solution left; there was no other way.

The Nuremberg Laws

The Nuremberg Laws of September 15, 1935 were necessary, the public was told, "for the protection of German blood and German honor." By order of Hitler, these laws were placed before the National Socialist Convention.

One law, the Reich Citizenship Law, discriminated between a subject of the State and a citizen of the Reich. Article two of that law stated: "A citizen of the Reich is only that subject who is of German or cognate blood and who, through his conduct, shows that he is both desirous and fit to serve faithfully the German people and the Reich." The law thus negated citizenship to Jews.

The second statute was the law for "Protection of the German Blood and of the German Honor." Among other things, this law set down that marriages between Jews and citizens of German or cognate blood were forbidden. Extramarital relations between Jews and citizens of German or cognate blood were forbidden. Jews were not to employ female citizens of German or cognate blood under forty-five years of age in their households. Jews were forbidden to hoist the Reich and national flags and to display the colors of the Reich.

A total of no less than thirteen regulations were published following the Nuremberg Laws, barring Jews from almost all positions and professions. The regulations also stipulated that the movements of the Jews were to be limited. These laws, however, were not the final delineation of Jewish status, as had been declared upon their acceptance in Nuremberg, but rather were only the beginning of the cruel repression sanctioned by means of the law. Under the Nuremberg Laws, two thousand people were sentenced during the years 1936 to 1939.

On April 26, 1938, nationwide registration of Jewish property was initiated. On June 14, 1938, all Jewish-owned businesses were to be registered and marked *Juedisches Geschaeft*. This was followed, on November 12 of the same year, by Aryanization or liquidation of Jewish-owned retail businesses, and on December 3, by liquidation of industrial enterprises and full-scale appropriation of Jewish property and businesses, leading to the pauperization of the Jewish population. Leipzig's Bruehl, the center of international fur trade, was especially hard hit at this time.

In addition, the Nazi regime enforced personal isolation and ostracism. The first census taken on a racial basis was held on May 17, 1938. Jews with German names were forced to adopt the added names of Israel or Sara on August 17, 1938. My own name, Solomon, was considered a Biblical name and the added name Israel was not required. I have often wondered why my father's name, Joseph, required the additional name Israel. Wasn't Joseph a Biblical name too? Perhaps the Nazis were not anxious to concede that Hitler's Propaganda Minister, Josef Goebbels, had a "Jewish" name!

In accordance with a decree on October 5, 1938, the letter J (*Jude*) was stamped on passports and identity cards. Compulsory identification cards were issued beginning on January 1, 1939, following a suggestion by Swiss authorities.

Thus, in a relatively short period, the German-Jewish community, which had numbered half a million in 1933, was reduced to less than half that number by 1939. By then, the Jews were considered to be outlaws who could expect nothing but continued harassment and persecution, and finally deportation to death.

BY 1936, EMIGRATION WAS PROCEEDING AT FULL TILT. The discussion among Jews was no longer whether one should leave,

We Prepare to Emigrate but rather to which country one should attempt to go. I was only nine years old when a poll on emigration was conducted in my class at the Carlebach Schule. Only one of the more than thirty students questioned responded that his family planned to remain in Leipzig for the time being. Only they felt that the situation would improve, or perhaps they had nowhere to turn.

Since our family owned a sewing machine, occasionally a tailor would come to our home to repair clothing. When my father inquired of him as to which country he was planning to immigrate to, his astonishing reply was that he was staying in Germany. He was not worried at all, he averred confidently. He was married to a Christian woman, and because of her, no Nazi would harm him. "I will be treated with kid gloves," he assured us.

I still remember my father strongly challenging his cocksure position. "If any harm should come to the Jewish community," my father told the tailor, "you will not be excluded. Hiding behind your Christian wife will not guarantee you safety and security. In Hitler's eyes, you are a Jew, no matter how far you distance yourself from the Jewish community. Your own Jewishness is all that matters to him." My father's message turned out to be prophetic indeed. Late in 1938, possibly in October or November, the tailor was arrested by Gestapo agents for reasons unbeknownst to me. When our family left Germany in April 1939, his whereabouts were still unknown. It should be pointed out that at the time of his arrest, mass deportations to concentration camps had not yet begun. The tailor's arrest and deportation was one of the earliest recorded in Leipzig.

❀ ❀ ❀

To assist Jewish community members with their plans to leave Germany, the *Gemeinde* announced a *Gemeinde Abend* at the Hoehere Israelitische Schule's gymnasium on May 19, 1936. The problems of emigration would be fully discussed and suggestions would be offered. The meeting featured Dr. A. Wachtel, an eminent authority on the subject of immigration, as the main speaker. Discussion among the audience would follow.

My parents attended this meeting and returned home with a firm decision to apply to the British consul for a certificate which would enable us to immigrate to Palestine. My parents fully agreed with the consensus at the meeting that some degree of anti-Semitism existed in every country, even in the best. "No one is really madly in love with the Jewish people," they stated. And who could predict the future of any country? Did any of the

Gemeindeabend.

Am **Dienstag,** 19. Mai, pünktlich 8.30 Uhr abends, findet in der Turnhalle der Höheren israelitischen Schule, Gustav-Adolf-Straße 7, ein

Gemeindeabend

statt, bei dem Herr Landgerichtsdirektor a. D. Dr. jur. **A. Wachtel,** Leipzig, Goethestraße 1, einen Vortrag über das Thema

„Planmäßige Auswanderung"

halten wird.

Hierzu laden wir unsere Gemeindemitglieder ergebenst ein und erwarten, da dem Vortrag das regste Interesse beizumessen ist, einen zahlreichen Besuch.

Leipzig, den 13. Mai 1936.

Der Vorstand der isr. Religionsgemeinde zu Leipzig.

Notice in the Gemeindeblatt announcing a forthcoming meeting to discuss
Jewish emigration from Leipzig

thousands of Jews who immigrated to Germany in the 1920s ever anticipate that the Germany of the Weimar Republic would in just a few short years become the Germany of Hitler? We thus felt that Palestine would be the safest haven for us.

It must be remembered that 1936 was the year of the Arab revolt in Palestine, which in reality was a campaign of violence directed at the Jews living there. Even though many Jews lost their lives at the hands of the Arab mobs, Palestine was still the first choice for a large segment of German Jewry. After all, this was *Eretz Yisrael,* our very own homeland.

Needless to say, I was overjoyed at this sudden turn of events. I had always dreamed of being in Palestine, and now that dream had become a real possibility. I enthusiastically launched into a self-study course of the Hebrew language. I was anxiously looking forward to my next encounter with the Nazi youth gangs, when I would be assaulted with their favorite slogan, *"Dreckicher Jude, raus von Deutschland! Warum fahrst du nicht nach Palaestina?"*

(Filthy Jew, get out of Germany! Why don't you go to Palestine?) I would then be able to answer proudly, "That was exactly where I was going!"

However, obtaining a certificate from the British was not a simple task. Certificates were issued only to individuals who were trained for specific types of labor, labor which was needed but lacking in Palestine. This presented quite a problem for many of Leipzig's Jews who earned their livelihoods as merchants and were engaged mainly in business activities.

My father's credentials proved to be totally inadequate. He had been trained as a *shochet*, but there was certainly no shortage of *shochtim* in Palestine. We also were the owners of a *Bestecke Geschaeft* (a silverware store), which also did not meet the British requirements for trained and skilled laborers.

My father then decided to learn a new profession. Masons, bricklayers, plumbers, electricians, carpenters, and painters were high on the list of priorities recommended by the British. With the anticipated increase in Jewish immigration to Palestine, many new buildings would have to be constructed. Therefore, workers in these fields would be of vital importance. My father thus chose to learn painting.

Though my father's instructor was reputed to be a first- class painter, he proved to be most unreliable. At first, my father spent much of his time searching for him. After a while, he discovered that the painter's favorite hideout was a bar on the Gerberstrasse. The man was always in a state of intoxication, even when he considered himself sober. However, he had never displayed any anti-Semitic tendencies, and was generally friendly toward the Jews. Most of his painting was done in Jewish homes. My father experienced a difficult few months before his instructor presented him with a diploma approved by Leipzig's League of Painters.

We soon discovered, however, that our aspirations to immigrate to Palestine would not be realized. The number of applications for certificates had grown tremendously, and the British would issue only a small number of certificates each month. It would take years before our turn came. My father then commented that he understood exactly how Moshe *Rabbeinu* felt when Hashem did not grant him the privilege of entering *Eretz Yisrael*. Sadly, my parents conceded that we must search for another country to accept us.

We pursued possibilities in several countries. Once, the *Gemeindeblatt* reported that the South American country of Chile was inclined to permit entry to Jews. Several weeks later, similar reports began to circulate regarding the Dominican Republic in Central America. None of these opportunities bore fruit, however, and my father finally wrote to his sister, Ettie Geisler, in Brooklyn. He explained the tragic situation of the Jews in Germany and told her why we must leave the country. A short time later, in November 1937, we received her affidavit, which would eventually enable us to immigrate to the United States.

UNDER THE LAW OF MARCH 31, 1938, supplemented by an order of October 6, 1938, Polish passports were revoked if their bearers

Deportation of the Polish Jews

had lived abroad for more than five years, unless a special visa had been issued by the consul. The Germans, with their own experience in racial legislation, instantly realized that this Polish stratagem was aimed at the Jews. After the law took effect on October 31, the Germans would risk being left with 15,000 stateless Jews whom no country would admit.

On October 26, the German ambassador was ordered to inform Warsaw that the Reich would proceed with the expulsion of Polish Jews from its territory unless the Poles formally undertook to permit them to return at any time without a special visa. When, on the following day, the Polish government refused to agree to this condition, an order was issued to the Gestapo to arrest everyone affected by the new Polish regulation and deport them surreptitiously into Poland before the law took effect.

❁ ❁ ❁

Zindel Grynszpan was a Polish Jew who owned a grocery store in the German city of Hanover. On April 25, 1961, at the Eichmann trial in Jerusalem, he described the expulsion:

> On Thursday night, October 27, 1938, at eight o'clock, a policeman arrived at our house and told us to come to Police Headquarters. He said that we would be returning shortly, so don't take anything with you except your passport.
>
> I went, accompanied by my wife, my son, and my daughter. At the police station we saw a large number of people, some sitting, some standing, and many crying. The police inspector was shouting, "Sign, sign, you are being deported." We all signed. We were then taken to a concert hall, where we saw people from all over Hanover. Approximately 600 people had assembled there. We remained there until Friday night, about 24 hours; yes, until Friday night. They then took us to the railroad station in police trucks, in prisoners' lorries, about 20 men in each truck. All along the way, people were shouting, "*Juden, raus zu Palaestina!*" The train took us to New Betscher on the German-Polish border. It was *Shabbos* morning, 6 a.m. when we arrived at New Betscher. Trains were arriving from many parts of Germany: from Leipzig, Berlin, Cologne, Duesseldorf, Essen, Bielefeld and Bremen. Altogether, about 12,000 people had arrived. When we reached the border, we were searched to ascertain the amount of money we were carrying. Since German law did not permit more than 10 Marks to be taken out of Germany, all monies in excess of that amount were confiscated by the Germans. The Germans said, "You

didn't bring any more with you when you came; you can't take out any more."

Grynszpan continued to relate that they were kept under constant guard and they were not permitted to communicate with anyone. They walked a little over a mile to the Polish border, where the Germans planned to smuggle them into Polish territory.

> The SS men were whipping us. Those who lingered were beaten and blood was flowing on the road. They tore our suitcases away from us. They treated us in a most brutal way. This was the first time that I had seen the wild brutality of the Germans. They shouted at us, "Run! Run!" I was struck down and fell into a ditch. My son came to my aid and said, "Run, father, run, or you'll die." When we reached the open border, the women went in first. The Poles knew nothing. They called a Polish general and some officers who examined our papers.
>
> When they saw we were Polish citizens and we had special passports, they decided to permit us to enter Poland.
>
> They took us to a village of about 6,000 inhabitants, although our group numbered 12,000. There was a heavy downpour. Some of the elderly among us were fainting. Our suffering was great. There was no food; since Thursday we had not eaten. We were then taken to a military camp and put in stables, as there was no room anywhere else. On Sunday, a truck arrived from Poznan with enough bread for all of us. The Grynszpan family was now in Zbonszyn.

The plight of the Jews in Zbonszyn was precarious indeed. A most vivid account appears in *Crystal Night* by Thalmann and Feinermann. A thousand Jews had arrived from Hamburg at seven in the morning, after twelve hours' travel. They were made to walk the last five miles to the frontier. The Polish guards confronted them with bayonets while the German police shoved them forward with their rifle butts, shouting, "Go on. Don't worry. They wouldn't dare shoot at you."

The guard fired into the air, at which the crowd of refugees panicked, knocked down the barriers and entered Poland. Physically and emotionally broken, they sat in the cold and rainy mud for three hours, nibbling on their last bits of food until they were authorized to proceed to Zbonszyn. In the inns, stables and sheds of this tiny village under Polish guard, they found thousands of other deportees who had already arrived.

At five in the evening, they were herded into the main square, where six officials sat behind tables to record their names and the names of any Polish friends or relatives who were likely to take them in. The crush was so great that the tables were knocked down and the officials gave up. They returned the next day and interviewed small groups at a time, treating them as foreigners and giving them no assistance.

The Parisian Yiddish daily paper *Pariser Haint*, in its November 4, 1938 edition, published a vivid account, written by the paper's correspondent in Zbonszyn, of the state of the deported Jews.

> Critical situation of Polish Jews deported from Germany. Thousands of Jews have overnight been rendered stateless. They were rounded up and deported largely to Zbonszyn, in a no-man's-land between Germany and Poland. Their living conditions are uncomfortable and distressing. Twelve hundred of them have fallen ill and several hundred are without shelter. As there is a risk of epidemic, Red Cross doctors with the help of doctors from the OSE (Oeuvre de Secours aux Enfants) have distributed typhus vaccinations and 10,000 aspirin tablets. A number of instances of insanity and suicide have been recorded.

❀ ❀ ❀

Friday, October 28, 1938, as far as our family was concerned, was to be a regular day, like all other days. I dressed and went to school. However, upon my arrival at school, I was astonished by how few of the students were in attendance. At approximately 9 a.m., it was announced that all school sessions that day had been officially canceled. We were advised not to linger on the streets and not to tarry. "Go directly to your homes and go as quickly as possible," we were urged. Needless to say, I was overjoyed. A day off from school; what could be better?

My usual route home was straight down the Gustav Adolf Strasse to the Humboldtstrasse, up to the Nordstrasse, where I turned left. It was a distance of almost one and a half kilometers. As I reached the intersection at the Pfaffendorfer Strasse (now Kurt Fischer Strasse), I saw my mother approaching. She was on her way to the school to take me home. She appeared to be quite nervous. She then informed me of the events of the day. All of Leipzig's Jews with Polish citizenship were being deported to Poland, she told me in a voice filled with shock and horror. No one was safe on the streets. We rushed home.

It must be noted at this time that although both my parents were born in Poland (Galicia), they had lost their Polish citizenship for various reasons and we were considered *statenlos* (stateless). Therefore, no imminent danger of deportation confronted us. We were apparently safe at this time.

When we arrived home, I immediately realized that my mother's older sister, Tante Hinde, a Polish citizen who lived with us, had already left. I was told that she was safe at the home of a friend who was *statenlos*. The Gestapo was not searching the homes of stateless Jews at this particular juncture.

All day Friday we remained at home, behind locked doors and drawn curtains. Since, like most of Leipzig's Jews, we did not own a radio, we received no news from the world outside.

Late in the afternoon, we were suddenly gripped by panic and trepidation when our doorbell rang. After much hesitation and discussion, my parents decided to open the door. Our state of terror

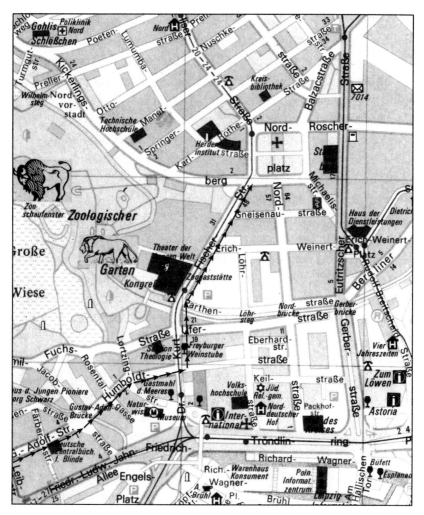

Streetmap of Leipzig's Jewish Section. The arrows trace the route taken.

was magnified even further when we saw Frau Tetzner standing there.

Frau Tetzner was a devout Catholic who, together with her husband, resided in the basement of our building. We had no choice but to invite her in. Little did we realize at that time that the Tetzners were surely of the *chassidei umos haolam*, of the righteous among the nations, who are destined to receive a share in the World to Come (*Tosefta Sanhedrin*, chapter 13 and *Maimonides, Laws of Repentance*, chapter 3.) They would be of great help to us in the coming weeks. The Tetzners played a prominent role in our survival and perhaps we owe our very lives to this wonderful couple.

Frau Tetzner had come simply as a friendly gesture to apprise us of the situation outside. She informed us that many Polish Jews had found, at least temporarily, a refuge on the premises of the Polish consulate. The grounds of the consulate were considered, by international law, to be sovereign Polish territory, and no Gestapo agent had the legal right to enter.

It seems that in the city of Halle on the Saale, just a short distance from Leipzig, deportation of Polish Jews had already commenced the evening before. Thus, when reports of these deportations reached Leipzig, many Polish Jews had ample time to reach the safety of the consulate before the Gestapo arrived at their homes.

Leipzig had always been a city where *Yiddishkeit* was felt in the very atmosphere. Anyone who observed the scene on the Nordstrasse on any given Friday and noticed all the hustle and bustle could readily conclude that it was *erev Shabbos*. On Friday, all the food stores were filled with customers doing their last-minute shopping for *Shabbos*. A pushcart peddler, selling fruits and vegetables, would appear each Friday on the corner of the Eberhardtstrasse and the Lomuehl Gasse, and many housewives would come out hunting for bargains. People could be seen carrying baking pans with kneaded dough shaped into *challos*. Since many families did not have their own baking ovens, these pans were taken either to the Schmeidler or the Scheinowitz Bakeries for professional baking. All day Friday, one could see men with towels under their arms heading for the *mikvah*. Everyone seemed to be preparing for *Shabbos*.

On Friday, October 28, 1938, however, the streets were empty and deserted. Very few Jews considered themselves safe out-of-doors. On that Friday evening we davened in the Bernstein Shul on Eberhardtstrasse 11, right around the corner from our house, and the usually packed *shtibel* had a much-diminished turnout. People generally preferred to remain in the security of their homes.

Services at the Broder Shul on Shabbos morning were concluded at a very early hour. Everyone was concerned with the situation developing at the Polish consulate. A huge multitude of Jews had taken refuge there, and the grounds were packed beyond capacity. There were hardly any food supplies available. Many people had been taken ill and the medical facilities were totally inadequate. The situation was desperate indeed.

In view of all this, the rabbis decided that a situation of genuine *pikuach nefesh* existed at the consulate. It now became the sacred obligation of each and every Jew not confined to the consulate, the stateless and those possessing German citizenship, to actively participate in the rescue effort of these unfortunate Jews. Operations must commence immediately.

Since food was vitally needed at the consulate, cooking and baking on this *Shabbos* was not merely permitted, but was mandatory according to *halachah*. All prohibitions concerning labor on *Shabbos* are suspended by the Torah itself when they are performed during life-saving endeavors, the rabbis ruled.

My mother had always been a scrupulous *Shabbos* observer. Therefore, watching her now, cooking and baking on *Shabbos*, had a profound effect on me. I began to fully comprehend the gravity of the situation. Suddenly, the dangers and uncertainties of our own existence became crystal clear to me. This, unfortunately, had not been the case in recent months.

When our planned immigration to Palestine had not materialized, I had developed a completely nonchalant attitude concerning emigration. I no longer had any desire to leave Germany. I simply did not care anymore. Perhaps, I reasoned, things will improve. I even remember cheering when the Austrian *Anschluss* was reported in March 1938. Typical of youths of my age, I was more concerned with the new Austrian soccer players who would now join the German national team than I was with the plight of my own people.

This attitude abruptly changed when I observed my mother working so feverishly and with such intense emotion to help improve the lot of some of our brethren at the consulate. My father's words of several weeks before were now ringing loudly and clearly in my ears. When I had suggested to him that things in Germany were bound to improve and that perhaps leaving the country was not really essential for us, I was emphatically told that we were going to the first country that would accept us. Now I was convinced. My father was right after all.

My mother said little that *Shabbos* as she worked with zeal and passion. The tears which occasionally rolled down her cheeks expressed her feelings and emotions much more eloquently than words ever could. She cooked, she baked *challos*, and she baked cakes. She used up every last ounce of flour in the cupboard. At approximately 2 p.m. we loaded up my younger brother's baby carriage and headed toward the Polish consulate. I can still recall the strange feelings and emotions which accompanied me as we wheeled the carriage cautiously through the streets of Leipzig.

The Polish consulate was located at the Villa Ury on the Waechterstrasse (now Dimitroffstrasse), quite a distance from our home. General Consul Chiczewski had rented this villa from the Jewish Ury family, which owned a large department store in Leipzig. Chiczewski was a gentile of outstanding virtue and morality.

Since the consul did not really own the villa, it had been the subject of debate as to whether it was legally considered extraterritorial — whether it was located outside the territorial limits of German jurisdiction. The consul apparently considered it sovereign Polish territory, and all Jews who contacted his office early on Friday asking for guidance in the deportation crisis were

Home of the Polish Consul, where 1,296 Polish Jews received temporary asylum.

instructed to come to his villa for safety and security. They would be the consul's guests. They would be granted asylum.

As we approached the Waechterstrasse, we noticed that the entire villa was ringed by police who interrogated all those seeking to enter. Furthermore, we noticed that the villa was in close proximity to the *Reichsgerichts* and *Polizeipraesidiums*. The police were thus close enough to be able to observe all activities at the Villa Ury from their office windows. It was, therefore, difficult to imagine how so many Jews were able to enter the grounds unmolested. Where were the police?

The police proceeded to check the identity cards of my parents, asked them several questions, and then permitted us to enter the villa.

The scene unfolding before our eyes was one of absolute horror and utter consternation. While we had expected to find two or three hundred Jews at the consulate, the number was probably closer to fifteen hundred. (The figure later confirmed by Leipzig's chief of police was 1,296.) Can one adequately portray the conditions prevailing when such a huge throng suddenly found itself confined to an area equipped to house thirty or forty people at most?

We noticed immediately that only standing room was available. People stood neck to neck and there was hardly any space for anyone to sit, even on the grass. Wheeling our carriage into the grounds proved to be a most arduous chore. And yet, these people had been standing there since early Friday morning, and it was now already *Shabbos* afternoon. Can anyone imagine the pain and suffering that these people were enduring? And there was no light at the end of the tunnel yet. No one knew how long the crisis would continue.

The food shortage at the consulate was most acute. Some people had not eaten since Thursday night. Consul Chiczewski had made an all-out effort to bring in more food from the outside, but it simply was not enough to feed 1,296 starving humans. The food supplies brought by the Jews were quickly exhausted. People were becoming weaker. Some were beginning to panic. How much longer could they survive?

Water was in ample supply. However, reaching the faucets proved to be quite a task. I abandoned my own quest for water when I noticed the distance to the nearest faucet and the multitudes of people blocking my path.

Sanitary facilities were horrendous. They certainly were not fit for civilized human beings. When one realizes that there were only eight lavatories available to accommodate the needs of approximately thirteen hundred people, one could well imagine their condition late that *Shabbos* afternoon.

The valiant efforts of Jewish doctors went a long way in averting a potential disaster. Though substantially hindered by the lack of medical supplies, these men labored at a feverish pace in the performance of their duties. Who knows how many lives were saved because of their extraordinary dedication to their work?

We spent two long hours at the consulate. What we saw was a two-hour human horror story. It was dreadful. How can I ever forget the pathetic faces pleading for assistance? Can I forget the elderly woman who collapsed before my very eyes or the agony and misery of so many defenseless individuals? Never had I witnessed such painful and vexing scenes. They will forever remain engraved in my mind.

When we left the consulate, two of the Bieder boys, Reuven and Yaakov, went with us. Since both were Polish citizens, we experienced some tense and anxious moments as we proceeded past the Nazi police guards. Fortunately, the crush was so great that no one questioned us about our nationality, and we were not asked to produce our identity cards.

By late *Shabbos* evening, the crisis was over. The German and Polish governments had worked out an arrangement whereby all Polish citizens could return to their homes without any fear of future deportation. However, they were required to register at the Polish consulate on October 31. Those who failed to register would be in danger of losing their Polish citizenship. In addition, on

Announcement requiring Polish citizens to register at their consulate.

November 1, they would have to register with the German police as foreign nationals.

In all, approximately five thousand of Leipzig's Jews had been deported to Poland, far more than from any other German city. This was due to the fact that the overwhelming majority of Orthodox Jews were *Ostjuden*. Seventy-three percent of Leipzig's Jews were foreign born; only seven percent of the members of the *Talmud Torah Verein* (which included the Otto Schill Strasse Synagogue, the Broder Shul, and many others) possessed German citizenship. Thus, most of the *Verein's* members were subjected to the deportation. Of the eighteen members of the *Religionsgemeinde's Vorstand*, twelve were of Polish origin. Thus, even before Kristallnacht, the activities of the *Gemeinde* came to a virtual standstill.

Those German Jews who found themselves in Poland after their deportation were in dire need of financial assistance. Their economic status can best be described as hopeless. They were generally a despondent group. They turned to every corner in their quest for immigration to other countries, but their search was in vain. No country would grant them entrance visas. No one wanted these (or indeed any) Jews. The doors had all been tightly shut.

At least, they felt, they were no longer under the yoke of Nazi oppression. How were they to know that this was only a temporary respite? Within ten months, on September 1, 1939, the Nazis fired the opening shot of World War II as their armies marched into Poland. Once again, these hapless Jews were subjected to Nazi persecution.

Meanwhile, in Zbonszyn, Zindel Grynszpan sent a letter to his seventeen-year-old son, Herschel, who had gone to live with an uncle in Paris. In this missive he described to his son his family's travails during the Polish deportation. This news plunged Herschel into deep despair. He was greatly pained by the news of his parents' deportation and, hoping to shock the world into action

Herschel Grynszpan

on behalf of the Jews, he became determined to shoot the German ambassador in Paris.

On November 7, early in the morning, he approached the German embassy. Several minutes after his arrival, Herschel was shown into Third Secretary Ernst vom Rath's office. He then fired five shots at vom Rath. Although grievously wounded, vom Rath was able to survive until the afternoon of November 9, when he lapsed into a coma. Later that day, the German Embassy issued the following statement: "Ernst vom Rath, recently appointed Embassy Counselor by the Fuehrer, died at 4:30 in the afternoon of wounds sustained from the attempt on his life of November 7."

A card which Herschel had written in his hotel room was found in his possession. He had written to his parents explaining his act, "I could not do otherwise. May G-d forgive me. My heart bleeds at the news of the suffering of thousands of Jews. I must protest in such a way that the world will hear me. I must do it. Forgive me."

To the public prosecutor Herschel stated, "I was not motivated by hatred or by vengeance, but by love for my father and my people, who have endured unbearable suffering. I deeply regret having injured anyone, but I had no other way of expressing myself."

After describing the nightmare lived by the Polish Jews in Germany, he added, "To be Jewish is not a crime. We are not animals. The Jewish people have a right to live!"

When the news of vom Rath's assassination reached Germany, the Jewish communities realized in horror what would be in store for them. In many synagogues, special prayer sessions were organized. Some recited chapters from the Book of Psalms around the clock.

Headlines in newspapers all over Germany blasted this act. The *Leipziger Neueste Nachrichten* reported "a cowardly Jewish murder in Paris" and "an act of hatred." Newspapers warned of severe consequences and of serious repercussions. "Jews must be taught a lesson!" shouted Goebbels' propaganda sheet, the *Voelkischer Beobachter*. "It is clear what conclusions Germans will draw from this latest event. We shall no longer tolerate the hundreds of thousands of Jews within our territory, who control entire streets of shops, who avail themselves of our public entertainments, and as foreign landlords pocket the wealth of German leaseholders while their brothers in religion incite war on Germany and assassinate German officials."

There could no longer be any doubt. Goebbels had spoken; the die had been cast. A pogrom was inevitable. No one, however, expected it to come so quickly and no one could have foretold its severity.

Last-minute attempts were made to persuade Neville Chamberlain's British government to use its influence with the Germans to suspend these imminent measures of retaliation against German Jewry, but the British refused to become associated with any support of German Jewry. Perhaps Chamberlain felt that doing so might jeopardize the "peace in our time" letter he received from Hitler in September 1938, when he handed Hitler the Czech Sudetenland on a silver platter.

What followed on November 9 and 10, 1938, was an orgy of arson, property destruction, and murder of Jews at a rate as yet unprecedented in Nazi Germany.

Four

Kristallnacht

HOUGH THE GERMAN GOVERNMENT ATTEMPTED to present these actions as a spontaneous protest of Germans in reaction to the murder of Ernst vom Rath, they were actually planned well in advance and unleashed on the evening of November 9, 1938 at the order of Nazi leaders, who congregated in Munich for the annual commemoration of Hitler's abortive Beer-Hall Putsch in 1923.

On November 10, at 1:20 a.m., Reinhard Heydrich flashed an urgent teletype message to all headquarters and stations of the police and the Gestapo, instructing them to organize the demonstrations. He ordered the burning of synagogues. Businesses and

The New York Times.

Copyright, 1938, by The New York Times Company.

Entered as Second Class Matter, Postoffice, New York, N. Y.   NEW YORK, FRIDAY, NOVEMBER 11, 1938.   P

NAZIS SMASH, LOOT AND BURN JEWISH SHOPS AND TEMPLES UNTIL GOEBBELS CALLS HALT

BANDS ROVE CITIES

Thousands Arrested for 'Protection' as Gangs Avenge Paris Death

The American press reports on Kristallnacht.

private apartments belonging to Jews were to be destroyed, and police were not to hinder the demonstrators. He ordered that in all districts, as many Jews were to be arrested as could be accommodated in existing prisons. Upon these arrests, the appropriate concentration camps should be contacted in order to confine the prisoners in these camps as quickly as possible. These teletyped instructions were carried out to the letter throughout Germany and Austria. The planned pogrom was a complete success.

As a result, Heydrich was able to report to Goering that 815 shops, 171 homes, and 76 synagogues were destroyed; 36 Jews were killed and 36 seriously injured; and 191 synagogues were burned. Some 20,000 Jews were arrested and sent to concentration camps, mainly the Buchenwald camp, in the vicinity of Weimar. Heydrich emphasized that since these reports were prepared on quick notice, the figures presented must have been exceeded considerably.

Leipzig shared the same fate as other cities. The fire department reported that on Thursday morning at 3:51, a fire alarm brought them to the Gemeinde Synagogue on the Gottschedstrasse, only to discover that the entire structure was already engulfed in flames. Since the fire was already too far advanced to save the synagogue, they concentrated all their efforts on preventing the fire from

The Gemeinde Synagogue, burning the morning after Kristallnacht.

spreading to neighboring buildings. The department listed the cause of the fire as "undetermined."

So much debris now covered the corner of the Gottschedstrasse and the Zentralstrasse that not only did it create traffic congestion of major proportions, but it also became a hazard to human life. Since Jews were considered to be ultimately responsible for the chaotic conditions that prevailed, Jews were forcibly recruited for the arduous task of cleaning up the accumulated debris. Driven by the police and jeered by onlooking spectators, they worked strenuously to fulfill the responsibilities suddenly cast upon them.

Yet another hazard existed at the Gottschedstrasse. Since all the synagogue's entrances were now wide open, Aryans could now roam freely within the skeleton that remained and search for souvenirs among the charred ruins. With the collapse of the entire framework of the building imminent, the *Polizeiamt* director hastily dispatched an urgent letter, dated November 11, 1938, to the *Religionsgemeinde* demanding the immediate barring of all entrances. Should there be a failure to comply with this demand, the police themselves would handle the matter at the *Gemeinde's* expense and a fine of 150 marks would be assessed against the *Gemeinde*.

The *Gemeinde's* response came on December 7. They asked that the fine be suspended on the grounds that on November 10, the *Gemeinde* had been closed by the authorities and that they, therefore, were totally unaware of the police's ultimatum. Only on the preceding day, December 6, when they had been permitted to reopen, did the police's letter reach their hands. I am not familiar with how this matter was finally resolved. However, I do know that the building was entirely demolished within the following several days. A short time later, my friend Reuven Bieder and I walked by the synagogue corner and found nothing but an empty lot.

At 5:05 on the morning of November 10, another fire was reported at the corner of Goethe Strasse and Grimmaische Strasse, where the Jewish firm of Bamberger and Hertz was located. When the firefighters arrived and discovered that the entire lower three floors had already been engulfed in flames, their main goal became the protection of the neighboring *Kaffeehaus Corso* and of the many Aryan business offices situated on the upper floors.

As for protecting neighboring buildings, I can personally testify that the firefighters fulfilled their assignment most capably. Several days after the fire, we scrutinized the area from the Augustus Platz (now Karl Marx Platz) right across the street. We saw what amounted to a straight vertical line separating Bam-

Israelitische Religionsgemeinde
zu Leipzig

Leipzig C 1, am 7.Dezember 1938.
Walter-Blümel-Straße 10¹
Fernsprecher Nr.
Postscheckkonto Nr.

Tagb.-Nr. 5031/31

Es wird gebeten, die Antwort nicht an
die Person des Unterzeichneten zu
richten und Briefbuch-Nr. anzugeben.

An den

Der Oberbürgermeister
-8.DEZ.1918
der Stadt Leipzig

Herrn Oberbürgermeister der
Reichsmessestadt L e i p z i g ,
Baupolizeiamt,

L e i p z i g .

Betr.: Ihr Zeichen BPA,Bez.I Gottsch. 3/38.

Wie dortseits bekannt sein wird, sind die Verwaltungs-
räume der israelitischen Religionsgemeinde zu Leipzig am 10. November 1938 behördlich geschlossen und erst am 6. ds.Mts. wieder
geöffnet worden. Die Auflage vom 11. vor.Mts. ist daher erst am
6. ds.Mts. in unsere Hände gelangt und konnte nicht erfüllt werden. Wir bitten deshalb, von der angedrohten Strafe abzusehen.
Die Gebühren werden demnächst überwiesen werden.

IsraelitischeReligionsgemeinde zu Leipzig
Verwaltung

*Religionsge-
gemeinde's
response to the
authorities,
as to why
they could not
comply with
the ultimatum
of the Polizeiamt
director*

berger and Hertz from its neighboring houses. The destruction
ended exactly at the very edge of the structure. It was truly an
amazing performance of firefighting.

The cause of the fire was listed as arson, and the accused
arsonists were the owners themselves. The allegation stated that
their purpose was to collect on their insurance policy. The owners'
arrest followed immediately.

On one of my two post-World War II visits to Leipzig, an
elderly German was attempting to impress me with his warm
attachment and devotion to Jews. This practice has become rather

The Jewish store, Bamberger and Hertz, burning, the morning after Kristallnacht.

fashionable in Germany nowadays. "When before Kristallnacht, my friends were planning the break-in at Bamberger and Hertz," he claimed, "I warned them of the impending consequences. 'This will become our ruination. The world will condemn us as outlaws.

It may yet involve us in a war.'

"Unfortunately," he continued, "my associates completely ignored my admonitions."

His wife sharply rebuked him. "Tell the truth," she said. "You warned no one. You yourself were one of the people who broke in and put it to the torch. You were equally guilty." "Now, wait a minute," I interjected. "Didn't the owners themselves start the fire?" The wife replied, "Do you really believe this Nazi propaganda?"

At 5:19, the fire engines made their way to the Hoehere Israelitische Schule, where they succeeded in extinguishing a small fire which caused minimal damage. Similar results were reported at the Jewish *Kaufhaus Ury* on the Koenigsplatz (now Wilhelm Leuschner Platz), where a fire was reported at 5:50.

The fire department arrived too late to save the Eitz Chaim Synagogue at the Otto Schill Strasse. The fire was reported at 5:20, and only the neighboring buildings were salvaged. All that we saw a short time later, as we proceeded through the area, was another empty lot. "What a shame," remarked Reuven Bieder. "Now we'll never see it again." This beautiful edifice, constructed in 1922, had lasted for only sixteen years. How sad!

At 11:07, a fire was reported at the *Israelitischen Friedhof* on the Delitzscher Landstrasse (now the D.S.F. Strasse in Eutritzsch). This was the newest of Leipzig's three Jewish cemeteries; its chapel had been dedicated only ten years before. Here again, the firefighters were successful in localizing the fire, preventing it from spreading to other areas. The chapel, however, was totally destroyed.

The destruction of the two large synagogues and the cemetery chapel brought in some welcome funds to fill Nazi coffers. Several days after Kristallnacht, an item appeared in Leipzig's newspapers offering 200,000 bricks for sale, bricks which apparently had been salvaged from the wrecked synagogues. In November 1942, the Nazis finally appropriated — in a perfectly legal manner, of course — the land on which the synagogues had stood.

Chapel at Leipzig's New Cemetery, which was totally destroyed during Kristallnacht.

All of Leipzig's synagogues felt the wrath of the Nazi hordes on that November 10 as they rampaged throughout the Jewish area. The synagogue on the Faerberstrasse was demolished beyond recognition. It appeared as if it had been hit by a tornado. Religious items, such as *siddurim, Chumashim,* and even the holy Torah scrolls were maliciously thrown into the street. Nothing was sacred to these barbarians.

When Rabbi Rogosnitzky attempted to recover some of these holy objects, he was arrested on the spot. There followed a beard-trimming ceremony on the corner of the Faerberstrasse and Gustav Adolf Strasse, in which a large portion of his beard was cut off. Some friends of ours witnessed this debasing act of abuse from

Ads, such as this one, appeared in Leipzig's newspapers, offering 200,000 used bricks for sale. These bricks were salvaged from Leipzig's destroyed synagogues.

Abbruch

Synagogen Gottschedstr. u. Apels Garten

ca. 200000 Mauersteine,

unabgeputzt, pro Mille 15.- RM, noch abzugeben. — Verkauf bei den Polleren.

H. Fr. Seydel, Baugeschäft, Tel. **550 84.**

their homes, peeking out from behind window shades and curtains. Soon thereafter, though, Rabbi Rogosnitzky was unexpectedly released from custody.

This bit of information was revealed by a German police officer after the war: the Broder Shul was saved from the flames in compliance with Heydrich's strict instructions to burn synagogues only as long as German life and property were not endangered. The *shul* was situated in such close proximity to so many Aryan residences that such safety could not be guaranteed in that case.

The Broder Shul building was thus spared the fate of the other synagogues, but it did not remain completely unscathed. It suffered the same fate as the Faerberstrasse synagogue. Not one inch of the *shul* was overlooked. Furniture was overturned and destroyed, windows were smashed, and sacred objects were desecrated in the most grotesque fashion.

The debris outside, on the Keilstrasse, was piled high and the street was a litter of shattered glass, smoldering ashes, torn holy books, and other broken sacred objects. Many were eventually taken home by a mob of spectators, who looted and plundered to their hearts' content. Others were put to the torch. My younger sister Rachel, who was nine years old at the time, still remembers the smoke beneath the debris even on the following day.

Leipzig's post-World War II *Religionsgemeinde* published a list of thirteen synagogues and *shtiblach* that existed in Leipzig in 1938. Since the *shtibel* of the Boyaner Rebbe and the Kolomeaer Shul do not appear on this list, and since my father had mentioned on numerous occasions that there were more than twenty houses of worship in Leipzig, I assume that the *Religionsgemeinde's* list is incomplete. In any event, every one of Leipzig's houses of worship had felt the heavy hand of the Nazis on Kristallnacht, and they all lay in ruins. Later, the synagogues were officially locked by the authorities, effectively ending all public Jewish prayer sessions, at least for the time being.

Anyone observing the scene on Leipzig's Bruehl on November

Ury's Kaufhaus (Department Store) after Kristallnacht — note the boarded-up show windows

10, 1938 certainly would have become perturbed by the chaotic and treacherous conditions prevailing. Shop windows had been smashed and their contents looted by plundering marauders. The Jewish victims were then coerced to participate in a street-cleaning operation, while onlookers jeered and displayed their general contempt of the Jews with words of derision and mockery. Similar scenes could also be observed in other streets in the Jewish section of Leipzig. Hardly a Jewish shop was overlooked in this well-prepared pogrom.

Between November 10 and November 15, 1938, a total of more

The barracks at the Buchenwald concentration camp.

than 550 of Leipzig's Jews were imprisoned on a series of trumped-up charges. The international *Lagerkomitee* in Buchenwald reported in June 1945 that 270 of the 10,500 Jews imprisoned there in November 1938 had come from Leipzig.

To the arresting Gestapo officers, neither age nor profession mattered. The prisoners ranged in age from 19 to 76. Among the prisoners one could find men of all walks of life. There were merchants, physicians, mechanics, furriers, and many men of other vocations. Rabbis David Ochs and Gustav Cohn were among the detainees.

Thus, in the brief period from June to December, 6,700 Jews were driven out of Leipzig. The Aryanization and liquidation of Jewish-owned retail businesses, followed by the deportation of Polish Jews and the arrests after the infamous *Pogromnacht*, were indeed gigantic steps toward the ultimate Nazi goal of making Germany *Judenrein*.

Following Kristallnacht, on November 21, the American consul in Leipzig, David H. Buffum, sent the following report on events there to the Consul General in Berlin:

The shattering of shop windows, looting of stores and dwellings of Jews which began in the early hours of November 10, 1938, was hailed subsequently in the Nazi press as "a spontaneous wave of righteous indignation throughout Germany, as a result of the cowardly Jewish murder of Third Secretary vom Rath in the German Embassy in Paris." So far as a very high percentage of the German populace is concerned, a state of popular indignation that would spontaneously lead to such excesses, can be considered as non-existent. On the contrary, in viewing the ruins and attendant measures employed, all the local crowds observed were obviously benumbed over what had happened and aghast over the unprecedented fury of Nazi acts that had been or were taking place with bewildering rapidity throughout their city.

The whole lamentable affair was organized in such a sinister fashion as to lend credence to the theory that the execution of it had involved studied preparation. It has been ascertained by this office that the plan of "spontaneous indignation" leaked out in Leipzig several hours before news of the death of Third Secretary vom Rath had been broadcast. It is stated upon authority believed to be reliable, that most of the evening of November 9th was employed in drawing up lists of fated victims. Several persons known to this office were aware at 9 p.m. on the evening of November 9th, 1938, that the "spontaneous" outrage was scheduled for that night sometime after midnight and several of such persons interviewed stayed up purposely in order to witness it.

At 3 a.m. November 10, 1938, a barrage of Nazi ferocity was unleashed that had had no equal hitherto in Germany or very likely anywhere else in the world. Jewish dwellings were smashed into and contents demolished or looted. In one of the Jewish sections, an eighteen-year-old boy was hurled from a three-story window to land with both legs broken on a street littered with burning beds, other household furniture, and effects from his family's and other apartments. This information was supplied by an attending physician. It is reported from another quarter, that among domestic effects thrown out of a Jewish dwelling, a small dog descended four flights to land with a broken spine on a cluttered street.

Although apparently centered in poor districts, the raid was not confined to the humble classes. One apartment of exceptionally refined occupants known to this office was violently ransacked, presumably in a search for valuables that was not in vain, and one of the marauders thrust a cane through a priceless medieval painting portraying a Biblical scene. Another apartment of the same category is known to have been turned upside down in the frenzied course of whatever the invaders were after. Reported losses to looting of cash, silver, jewelry, and otherwise easily convertible articles have been frequent.

Jewish shop windows by the hundreds were systematically and wantonly smashed throughout the entire city at a loss estimated at several millions of marks. There are reports that substantial losses have been sustained on the famous Leipzig Bruehl, as many of the shop windows at the time of the demolition were filled with costly furs that were seized before the windows could be boarded up. In proportion to the general destruction of real estate, however, losses of goods are felt to have been relatively small. The spectators who viewed the wreckage when daylight arrived were mostly in such a bewildered mood that there was no danger of impulsive acts, and the perpetrators probably were too busy in carrying out their schedule to take off a lot of time for personal profit. At all events, the main streets of the city were a positive litter of shattered plate glass. According to reliable testimony, the debacle was executed by SS men and Storm Troopers not in uniform, each group having been provided with hammers, axes, crowbars, and incendiary bombs.

Three synagogues in Leipzig were fired simultaneously by incendiary bombs and all sacred objects and records desecrated or destroyed, in most instances hurled through the windows and burned in the streets. No attempts whatsoever were made to quench the fires, functions of the fire brigade having been confined to spraying water on adjoining buildings. All of the synagogues were irreparably gutted by flames and the walls of the two that were in close proximity of the Consulate are now being razed. The blackened frames have been the centers of attraction during the past week of terror for eloquently silent and bewildered crowds.

One of the largest clothing stores in the heart of the city was destroyed by flames from incendiary bombs; only the charred walls and gutted roof have been left standing. As was the case with the synagogues, no attempts on the part of the fire brigade were made to extinguish the fire, although apparently there was a certain amount of apprehension for adjacent property, for the walls of a coffee house next door were covered with asbestos and sprayed by the doughty firemen. It is extremely difficult to believe, but the owners of the clothing store were actually charged with setting the fire and on that basis were dragged from their beds at 6 a.m. and clapped into prison.

Tactics which closely approached the ghoulish took place at the Jewish cemetery where the temple was fired together with a building occupied by caretakers, tombstones uprooted and graves violated. Eyewitnesses considered reliable report that ten corpses were left unburied at this cemetery for a week's time because all gravediggers and cemetery attendants had been arrested.

Ferocious as was the violation of property, the most hideous phase of the so-called "spontaneous action" was the wholesale arrest and transportation to concentration camps of male German Jews between the ages of 16 and 60, as well as Jewish men without citizenship. This has been taking place daily since the night of horror. This office has no way of accurately checking the numbers of such arrests, but there is very little question that they have gone into several thousands in Leipzig alone.

Having demolished dwellings and hurled most of the movable effects to the streets, the insatiably sadistic perpetrators threw many of the trembling inmates into a small stream that flows through the Zoological Park, commanding horrified spectators to spit at them, defile them with mud, and jeer at their plight. The latter incident has been repeatedly corroborated by German witnesses who were nauseated in telling the tale. The slightest manifestation of sympathy evoked a positive fury on the part of the perpetrators and the crowd was powerless to do anything but turn horror-stricken eyes from the scene of abuse, or leave the vicinity. These tactics were carried out the entire morning of November 10th without police intervention and they were applied to men, women and children.

There is much evidence of physical violence, including several deaths. At least half a dozen cases have been personally observed, victims with bloody, badly bruised faces having fled to this office, believing that as refugees their desire to emigrate could be expedited here. As a matter of fact, this Consulate has been a bedlam of humanity for the past ten days, most of these visitors being desperate women, as their husbands and sons had been taken off to concentration camps.

This report is indeed a most graphic and vivid account of the Leipzig scene on November 10, 1938. It expresses the grave concern of the Consulate about the savage treatment of a segment of German society. However, one must take issue with one particular impression conveyed by the report.

The report states that "all" local crowds were obviously

TELEGRAM RECEIVED

FROM

JR
This telegram must be
closely paraphrased be-
fore being communicated
to anyone. (br)

Leipzig

Dated November 10, 1938

Rec'd 8:40 a.m.

Secretary of State,

Washington.

November 10, 11 a.m.

Violent anti-Semitic ~~pogrom~~ in progress in

Leipzig. Three synagogues in flames one next Consulate

burning but fire under control. Hundreds of shop

windows throughout city smashed no American property or

lives molested as yet. Fur district badly damaged.

HTK:DDM   BUFFUM

Telegram dispatched to Washington by the U.S. Consul, reporting on Kristallnacht

"benumbed" over what had happened. It further states that horrified spectators were "commanded" to jeer at the plight of the victims.

I discussed this subject with my parents over and over again. We all had witnessed mob scenes of Nazis participating in such atrocities as portrayed by the Consulate. Never had we noticed any spectators "benumbed" over any of the heinous outrages performed. The spectators generally chose to participate of their own free will, and they acted with much enthusiasm and fervor. None of the spectators had to be "commanded" to jeer, to deride, and to mock the plight of the victims. Any German, even one vehemently opposed to Nazi barbarism, certainly would not have displayed such opposition in public, thus jeopardizing himself and his family. To state otherwise, and thereby whitewash and exonerate, even partially, some of the Nazis of the time, does not do justice to the historic record of the period.

Does that mean that there were no decent Germans who were unalterably opposed to, and even despised, the Nazi treatment of the Jews? Of course not. However, as stated, these Germans (few and far between) were generally too fearful, and thus reluctant, to proclaim their feelings publicly.

In the days following Kristallnacht, almost one hundred Aryan Germans were imprisoned on the charge of pro-Jewish solidarity. Professor Alfred Menzel, a learned Christian scholar, was sentenced to a long prison term. His major crime was the fact that he had taught at the Hoehere Israelitische Schule for many years and was generally sympathetic and supportive of Jewish causes. There were many others as well.

Herr Lieberman, a devout Christian salesman, was a regular customer at our silverware store. However, he never entered directly into the store, which had a sign clearly displayed stating, *Juedisches Geschaeft*. Instead, he would come to our apartment, which was contiguous to the store. One had to descend no more than four or five steps from the apartment to reach the store. Though he was quite fearful of the consequences should his sympathetic attitude toward Jews become exposed, he once informed us that he would not permit Hitler to turn him into a monstrous anti-Semite. Therefore, he stated, he would continue to shop at our store. Unfortunately, there were not too many Herr Liebermans to be found in Leipzig any more.

Being avid soccer fans, Reuven Bieder and I often attended soccer matches in Leipzig's stadiums. Once (perhaps in 1937 or 1938) during a visit of the D.S.C. (Dresdner Sport Club) for a game against "Tura Leipzig," we attempted to obtain an autograph from the D.S.C. superstar, Helmut Schoen, who was also a regular member of the German National team. (After World War II, Schoen became the captain of Germany's National team.)

Wearing our brown caps from the Carlbach Shule, we naturally stood out as Jews and, as a result, were subjected to much hassling from Nazi youths. A violent skirmish was prevented solely through the prompt intervention of Helmut Schoen, who proceeded to scold the perpetrators for their disgusting behavior. I can still recall his kind and comforting words to us that afternoon. He appeared genuinely concerned with our plight as Jews. This contrasted rather sharply with the attitude of most other German soccer players who generally treated us with utter disdain.

❦ ❦ ❦

When our family went to bed on Wednesday night, November 9, 1938, we had no inkling of what was in store for us on Thursday. If my parents were aware of anything, they did not share this information with me.

Sometime between 5:30 and 6 a.m., we were awakened by hysterical screams originating from outside our house. When my mother looked out the window to determine the source of the screams, she was startled to see that a huge mob of perhaps two hundred had gathered at the corner of the Nordstrasse and Eberhardtstrasse and was viciously and iniquitously assaulting Herr Karger, an elderly Jew with a long, white flowing beard, who was the proprietor of the restaurant on the corner.

My mother immediately telephoned the police to apprise them of the mob scene, one of major proportions, and state that immediate police involvement was essential. The response of the police was quite abrupt. Scenes similar to the one she was witnessing on her street, my mother was told, had been occurring all night long throughout Germany. The perpetrators were so numerous that the police were no longer able to cope with the situation. My mother hung up, realizing that no police protection would be forthcoming and that for all practical purposes, we were on our own. I was greatly frightened, perhaps expecting the worst.

Seconds later, my aunt Hinde Kaufteil and my younger sister rushed into the room. My aunt was panic-stricken. By now, the mob had assembled right in front of our store. Since her bedroom faced the street, she was able to clearly hear someone shouting, "Here's Kaufteil, let's get started." Within seconds, bricks were thrown through the shop window and moments later, our store was filled with maniacs, frantically screaming, *"Tod zu den Juden!"* (Death to the Jews!) At the same time, the madmen helped themselves to any of the store's merchandise their wicked hearts desired.

I was convinced that they would be in our house at any moment. But they didn't come. We heard the sound of barking dogs coming from the store, and suddenly — utter silence. Where was the mob? we wondered. Why weren't they here? We dressed quickly. We soon realized, though, that the mob had departed, perhaps to wreak havoc on another Jewish family. But why did they stop short of our house?

The solution to our mystery was not long in coming. The Tetzners owned at least ten trained dogs who performed at local circuses; that is how the Tetzners earned their livelihood. As soon as they heard the commotion outside, followed by the break-in at our store, they brought the dogs to the scene and their barking apparently terrified the mob and drove them away.

We soon discovered that most of the store's merchandise, some

Our silverware store on the Nordstrasse, which was looted by Nazi thugs on Kristallnacht. The windows on either side are those of our apartment.

quite valuable, had not been stolen. Obviously the hoodlums had left rather hurriedly and thus were unable to fully accomplish their mission, which included looting and plundering. Therefore, it was the consensus among all present that they would soon return, and we had no choice but to go into temporary hiding. We were pleasantly surprised to discover that not only the Tetzners, but another Aryan, our landlord, Herr Dillinger, were prepared to assist us wherever possible.

My younger brother and sister went to the Dillinger apartment on the third floor, while my parents, my aunt, two other women whose names I don't recall, and I went to the cellar, adjacent to the Tetzner apartment. It was approximately 6:30 a.m. when we descended to the cellar, and we were to remain there until the afternoon. My mother stuffed four rolls into my pockets. "We have no idea how long we'll have to remain in the cellar," she said, "and you may become hungry."

Lack of food never really became a problem for us in the cellar. Who had an appetite? We were much more concerned with our plight. When would this pogrom end? How long would we have to remain in this dingy place? What were the prospects for tomorrow?

Frau Tetzner not only kept us informed of outside developments, but she also brought us fruit, vegetables, hard-boiled eggs, and most importantly, water. She was familiar with our *kashrus* requirements, and therefore knew that she could not offer us anything prepared in her kitchen.

Meanwhile, the Nordstrasse, right near our home, had become the center of mob activities. We could hear the intensity and the volume of the noise right through the building walls. We felt trapped in the cellar. Emotionally, we felt as if we were confined to the dungeon of a large prison. "Could any real concentration camp be any worse than this?" I asked myself.

Several times that morning, certain "unknown" people came to search for my father. Our landlord, Herr Dillinger, stationed himself in front of the house and informed all inquirers that the Schapiras* had left earlier in the day to an unknown destination, maintaining this stance despite the fact that he was well aware of our hiding place. With a Nazi *Hakenkreuz* button pinned to his lapel, he was, naturally, believed and the search for my father was thus terminated.

Frau Tetzner's continual news reports from the outside brought us no solace. Furniture from Jewish homes was being hurled out of windows. The Nordstrasse and all adjacent streets were littered with demolished household items. Jews were being dragged from their homes and pushed underneath a bridge crossing the Parthe River. For what purpose? Frau Tetzner had no idea. Rumors began circulating that eventually the bridge would be blown up and the more than 150 Jews underneath would be crushed in the ruins. Fortunately, this did not materialize. (The events at the Parthe River are vividly depicted in Consul Buffum's report to the Consul General.)

After several hours in the cellar, the news began to improve. Frau Tetzner informed us that a representative of the United States Consulate had arrived at the Parthe River, and when he witnessed the subhuman treatment of the Jewish victims, he lodged an official complaint on behalf of the United States government. As a result, the victims were released. I cannot, however, vouch for the accuracy of the consul's positive involvement in this horrendous situation. Perhaps the consul's presence was merely a rumor which circulated at the time.

In the summer of 1990, I returned to the Nordstrasse and the Parthe. A monument has been erected to commemorate the tragic events of the Holocaust. I was emotionally overwhelmed when, upon measuring distances, I realized that in our hiding place, we were only a short distance from the center of a major pogrom,

---

* Since my paternal grandfather in Galicia had never obtained a civil marriage license, German authorities considered my father to be an illegitimate child. As a result, he was forced to adopt his mother's maiden name, Schapira or Szapira.

*Monument at the
Parthenstrasse
commemorating
Nazi atrocities.*

where so many Jews were tortured and tormented.

Later in the morning, the Dillingers brought my brother and sister down to the cellar. Their daughter had telephoned that she was coming to visit, and the Dillingers were concerned about their daughter's reaction to their harboring of Jews — even such innocent youngsters as my six-year-old brother and my nine-year-old sister.

As the day progressed, the situation on the Nordstrasse gradually returned to normal. By early in the afternoon, the mobs had dispersed and a calm and serene atmosphere prevailed. Frau Tetzner gave us the all-clear signal and we decided to leave the safety of the dingy cellar and return to our apartment.

Much to our astonishment, we found that no German had entered our store or our apartment. We found them exactly as we had left them. Nothing appeared to be missing, despite all the Nazi hordes who had been roaming the streets looting, plundering, and pillaging. Hardly a Jewish house existed on the Nordstrasse and adjacent streets which had not been violated by the Nazi mobs. How had our apartment managed to miss the brunt of Nazi wrath?

We were later informed that the Tetzners' dogs had guarded both our store and apartment faithfully. Any intruder had second thoughts when he was confronted by these barking animals. When my parents attempted to thank the Tetzners for their concern and kindness, the Tetzners refused to accept the credit. "You are religious people," Frau Tetzner told my parents. "You believe in G-d. Just say that your G-d helped you," she suggested. My parents wholeheartedly endorsed her suggestion.

A relative peace and tranquility returned to the streets of Leipzig. German police were again patrolling the Jewish section in large numbers. We were no longer on our own. Although the store window had not yet been replaced, and thus both the store and the apartment were not securely locked, we went to sleep that night content that the pogrom appeared to have ended, and with the help of *Hashem*, we were still healthy and alive.

On the following morning, Friday, November 11, our doorbell rang early. After some initial alarm and concern as to who might be there so early, we opened the door. Ruth Brenner, the twelve-year-old daughter of the proprietors of a chicken market, had come to inform my father that his services as a *shochet* would be needed that day. Since no chickens had been slaughtered on Thursday, much work remained for my father to perform on Friday, which was usually a slow day for *shochtim*.

❀ ❀ ❀

I often marvel at the great courage displayed by Leipzig's Jews. Synagogues are burned; others are demolished. Those that can be renovated and refurbished are ordered closed by the Nazi authorities. But what did the Leipzigers do? They organized illegal *minyanim* in private homes. Is that not a sign of courage and tenacity?

My father and I attended *Shabbos* services that week at the Uhrmacher home on the Keilstrasse. All possible precautions were taken to avoid detection by the Nazis. In order not to arouse suspicion, no more than two people at a time would enter and leave the house. Everything appeared safe and secure at the time. Now, fifty-two years later, it seems incredible to me to have performed such services right under the noses of the Nazis who had strictly outlawed them.

Leipzig's Jews were determined that daily public services be revived. On November 25, thirteen members of the Tiktiner Shul signed a letter sent to the *Polizeipraesidium* of Leipzig. As Polish citizens, they requested that their synagogue, which had been closed by the authorities, be permitted to reopen for daily services. Though their request was denied, it was nevertheless a display of a courageous and daring spirit and contempt for danger. When one considers the Germans' hysterical animosity toward the Jews, such a letter could well have incited the Nazis to further physical violence.

Eventually, two *shuls* were permitted to reopen. One was the *Vierundzwanzig* on the Humboldtstrasse and the other, to the best of my recollection, was the Bochner Shul on the Gerberstrasse. Needless to say, both *shuls* were usually packed to the rafters. I distinctly remember that the *Vierundzwanzig* organized as many as four or five *minyanim* to take place at different times to accommodate the many worshipers who streamed through its doors.

Oppression of Leipzig's Jews never seemed to cease, however. As soon as the Kristallnacht pogrom ended, the Jews were faced

Leipzig, d. 25 Nov.1938

An das

Polizeipräsidium

Leipzig

Leipzig

Die unterzeichnete polnische Staatsangehörige
erlauben sich hiermit zu bitten Ihnen den Gottes-
Dienst in Tiktiner Synagoge, Richard Wagnerstr, 3
wie früher täglich abhalten zu gestatten.
Das Bethaus wurde am 24 Nov.1938 behördlich geschlossen.

Letter sent to the Lepzig Police authorities, requesting permission to reopen the Tiktiner Shul.

with the problem of new arrests. This time, German citizens and the stateless were the targets. Men were surreptitiously arrested at their homes and led away without being able to leave any notification to their loved ones as to their destination. Rumors were rampant as to their whereabouts. It was generally assumed that they were taken to concentration camps, places on earth from where no one returned alive.

My father did not stay around long enough to find out. Since the homes of Polish citizens were considered safe at that time, he left home and for the next several days, our friends the Baums graciously extended him their hospitality. Occasionally, I was able to see my father during the daytime as he made his usual rounds to the chicken markets.

Although I am not quite sure as to how often the Gestapo visited our home in search of my father, I do recall at least one such occasion. I can still remember the Gestapo agent searching through every nook and cranny of our apartment. He looked through the closets and even underneath the beds. I was not worried because I knew my father was not there. But, of course, my father was nowhere to be found. My mother pretended total ignorance of his whereabouts. The agent discussed the fact that so many Jews had been smuggled into Belgium, and suggested that perhaps my father was one of those Jews. My mother, however, remained adamant. She simply did not know. We all had the strong feeling that the agent left our house convinced that my father was by then in Antwerp, Belgium.

With my father no longer at home, some neighbors felt that it was unsafe for us to spend the night in our apartment. Many German hoodlums now roamed the streets of the Jewish neighborhood searching for the spoils of Kristallnacht, and our apartment, without the presence of an adult male, presented a most vulnerable target. Although the store window had by now been boarded up, the boards certainly could not serve as a deterrent for a thug determined to possess a share of Jewish property.

So the family split up. The following night, my mother, my aunt and my sister went to the *Hinterhaus* of Eberhardtstrasse 10, where for the next several nights they were the guests of Frau Kraemer, and my brother and I went to the third-floor apartment of the Bieder family, right across the street from our home.

How sad it was as I looked out the window and observed our house across the street! The store was boarded up. We no longer had a business. Our home no longer offered us safety and security. Our family was now scattered in three different locations. People were being dragged from their homes and sent to concentration camps. My father, too, was not immune from arrest. The streets were not safe for any of us. Wherever we went, we were subject to harassment. Nobody cared about us. Nobody wanted us. How much longer could we endure such an existence? With tears rolling down my cheeks, I called it a day.

As it turned out, our neighbors' concern for our safety was valid indeed. Several times during our absence from our home, total strangers rang the bell to our apartment in the wee hours of the morning. Each time, they were driven away by the Tetzners' dogs.

During my last trip to Leipzig, I attempted to locate the Tetzners to express my most sincere thanks and appreciation for their efforts in our behalf. Much to my dismay, I could find no trace of them.

As my friend Reuven Bieder and I leisurely walked down the Bruehl one day in late November, we were suddenly confronted with a truly horrifying scene. A large crowd had gathered to observe the proceedings. A group of twenty or twenty-five Jews were on their knees, each with a brush, a pail of water, and soap. Their specific assignment was to wash the sidewalk, the very same square yard of sidewalk, over and over again. While they were discharging their duties, they were constantly kicked by SS men, they were defiled with mud, and they were jeered and ridiculed by the spectators. At one point, when an SS officer poured a pail of water upon one of the victims, the excited onlookers cheered, and demanded more of the same.

When I asked Reuven how people could be so heartless to so cruelly abuse innocent human beings, I really wasn't expecting an answer. His answer, however, startled me, though it does contain a certain element of truth. "They are simply having fun," my friend said. "Unfortunately, torturing Jews is their 'sick' way of having fun."

Five

Leaving Leipzig

ARLY IN DECEMBER, SADNESS TURNED TO JOY in our home. Excitement reigned as we finally received the long anticipated letter from the United States consul in Berlin. The letter officially informed us that our application to immigrate to the United States had been tentatively approved. Our entire family was to appear at the American consulate in Berlin on February 15, 1939 for physical examinations. Should we satisfactorily pass these examinations, we would be eligible to receive visas to enter the United States as permanent residents.

This letter proved to be a lifesaver. We now knew that with the help of *Hashem*, we would, after all, survive this raging inferno of the so-called "master race." We would be able to continue to live normal lives as Jews.

January 1939 marked the date of the second deportation of Leipzig's Polish Jewish citizens. According to the *Gemeinde's* figures, more than a thousand Jews were involved in this nightmare. Included in this deportation was one of my classmates, whose name I sadly can no longer recall. Eight months later, with the German conquest of Poland, these unfortunate Jews again fell under the yoke of Nazi oppression.

Although emigration from Germany had been progressing at a rapid pace ever since the adoption of the Nuremberg laws, after Kristallnacht emigration turned to flight with the Jews in a desperate search for countries which would permit them to enter. Almost daily, one could see huge lifts being packed with furniture and other belongings for Jews participating in the mass exodus. At this point, no one intended to remain in Germany, where terror was on the constant increase.

The story of the "new" Heinz Kogel clearly illustrates the rapid increase of hostility and animosity toward the Jews. Heinz Kogel resided on the Eberhardtstrasse, a lone Christian youngster on a block with approximately twenty Jewish children his age. His mother displayed no anti-Semitic tendencies, and Heinz happily played with the Jewish children. He was considered to be one of the boys. We treated him kindly and he always felt right at home with us.

After Kristallnacht, however, his family moved to another area. Sometime in January, Reuven Bieder and I saw Heinz on the Bruehl in the company of a group of his Christian friends. He was wearing the uniform of the Nazi Youth Movement. When he saw us from a distance, he immediately began shouting the familiar slogans we had become so accustomed to: "*Verfluchte Juden! Schmutzige Juden!*" These slogans coming from the mouth of

Heinz Kogel, though, startled us. What had happened to him during the span of two short months?

We had no choice but to engage him in conversation. When I informed him that we were moving to America, he began to scream hysterically. "Just wait," he told us. "Our armies will soon be marching victoriously through the streets of New York. *Heute Deutschland, morgen die ganze Welt!* (Today Germany, tomorrow the entire world!) You cannot escape from us. Once and for all, we will rid the world of the Jewish cancer which has contaminated it ever since the beginning of history. *Deutschland, Deutschland ueber alles!"*

We realized that any attempt to reason with our brainwashed "friend" would be futile. His mind was already made up In addition, we were fearful that further discussion might initiate a violent physical encounter which could have undesired repercussions. So we peacefully came to a parting of the ways.

One must marvel at the superb job of indoctrination performed by the Nazi Youth Movement under the effective leadership of Baldur von Schirach, the Third Reich's First Youth Leader. In just two months, they had succeeded in transforming Heinz Kogel from a youth of warmth and compassion into an abominable creature filled with hatred and hostility. Unfortunately, there were many such "Heinz Kogels" throughout Germany.

Von Schirach, who later became the *gauleiter* of Vienna, was eventually sentenced at the Nuremberg trials to twenty years' imprisonment.

Meanwhile, unscrupulous, ambitious taxi drivers utilized these hard hours of Jewish adversity to their own financial advantage. Almost on a daily basis, they circulated rumors that certain consulates in Leipzig had consented to grant visas to the first ten or twenty applicants. Since hardly anyone owned a private car and public transportation was generally slow and unreliable, hundreds of Jews would rush into taxis to be among the first applicants. One can well imagine their feelings of disappointment and frustration when they discovered that the rumors were nothing but hoaxes.

❧ ❧ ❧

On Friday, February 10, just five days before our scheduled appointment with the American consul in Berlin, we received a letter from the consul notifying us that our scheduled appointment on the 15th had been cancelled. We were assigned a new quota number, one which would not be reached before 1943.

This letter hit us like a bomb. How could we possibly survive in Germany for four more years, when each single day was a nightmare? We were emotionally overcome. We became depressed and dejected. Why were the Americans doing this to us? We had been led to the brink of freedom only to be returned to torture and persecution.

My father traveled to Berlin on the following Monday, February 13, to discuss our problem with the leaders of several Jewish organizations. He soon discovered that other Jews had received similar cancellations in the past. Yet, when they kept their original appointments, they were nevertheless issued visas for the United States. It was therefore suggested that we ignore the letter of the previous Friday and appear at the consulate the following Wednesday as originally scheduled.

Early Wednesday morning we made our way to Berlin in a most apprehensive frame of mind. At the appointed hour, a secretary entered the waiting room and announced the names of all people who were scheduled for examinations that day. One can well imagine our dismay when she returned to her office without having mentioned our names. However, she returned almost immediately and added our names to the list. What a relief! It certainly appeared that we were right on target again.

Needless to say, we were overjoyed when later in the day, the Consul General informed us that since we had met all the requirements, our visas to the United States would be mailed to us on March 1st. Despite some anti-Semitic remarks addressed to us on the train back to Leipzig, it was a most pleasant ride. Who cared what the Nazis said to us? We were on our way to America!

Our visas finally arrived on Friday, March 3, 1939, just two days before the joyous holiday of Purim. That, for us, truly proved to be a *Yom Tov* to remember.

Early in March, the Hoehere Israelitische Schule, which had been closed by the authorities since November 10, was permitted to reopen. One noticed immediately that there was a substantial reduction in the number of students attending. This was obviously due to the fact that so many families had left the country since the events of the previous November.

Dr. Weikersheimer, who had assumed the school's principalship upon Rabbi Carlebach's immigration to Palestine in 1936, addressed our class on the first day of school. He suggested that education was even more vital for us in troubled times. He was confident that because of the small sizes of the classes at the school, its educational facilities would even further improve and the remaining students would greatly benefit from them.

However, this attempt to motivate the students and give them added incentive to learning did not have the intended results. My classmates were all too preoccupied with their forthcoming immigration to other countries and displayed little interest or craving for any learning at all. This lack of interest was especially prominent in classes studying German language. Our instructor, Dr. Herman, was quite cognizant of this lackadaisical attitude of her students, but she was simply unable to cope with it. A student once specifically asked her why we should be studying German grammar when everyone was planning to leave the country. Her half-hearted response that German was one of the world's major languages and was spoken by intellectuals in many countries did not arouse anyone to a major commitment.

As I reflect upon these events now, more than fifty years after they occurred, I still fail to comprehend why so much effort and energy were expended to teach German grammar. Unless the school was so mandated by Leipzig's educational departments or unless this subject was required to maintain the school's accreditation, why was such great emphasis placed on studying a language which, for all practical purposes, was to become virtually extinct for the overwhelming majority of students at that time? This, of course, is in no way intended to be a critique of the personal qualities and capabilities of Dr. Herman, who was a wonderful human being, a gracious and affable lady.

Although one must distinguish between the German people of the Nazi period and their language, for it was the people, rather than the language, whose conduct was so cruel and savage, nevertheless, I seemed to develop a feeling of disdain for the language itself. When I recall all the abuse and disparaging remarks hurled at me and my fellow Jews by means of this language, the language itself almost appears to my subconscious to have actually participated in these crimes. I even become annoyed and irritated in hearing the polite *"Danke schoen"* or *"Bitte schoen"* when expressed by elderly Germans who, not so long ago, utilized the same German language not to express courtesy and civility, but rather to heap fire and brimstone upon their helpless victims.

In March 1939, the most popular subject taught at the Hoehere Israelitische Schule was the English language, ably taught to us by Dr. Gruenewald. Even those not planning to immigrate to an English-speaking country were most anxious to learn it.

Friday, March 31, was the final school day before our Pesach vacation. I knew that for me, it would be my last day ever at the school. As I said my final good-byes to teachers and classmates, I could not help but notice some unusually sad faces among my friends. I soon realized that these were the faces of those youngsters who as yet had no prospects of leaving Germany. They would have to remain indefinitely and await an uncertain future.

The school continued to function despite the steady decrease in the number of students, until finally, in June 1942, it was officially closed by the Nazi authorities.

Meanwhile, in our home, an important decision had to be made. With Pesach just a month away, should we leave for the United States now or should we postpone our voyage until after the holidays? Since in Germany we were exposed to constant danger and our very lives were imperiled, logic would mandate an immediate departure. However, there were yet other points to consider, and they eventually formed the basis for our final decision.

For one, our belongings had to be packed into a lift or into large crates for transportation to the United States, and this could not be accomplished on such short notice. In addition, passage on an ocean liner had to be booked. Since my father insisted on sailing on an American ship and we were thus bound by the schedules of the U.S.-German Lines, this presented us with a problem. Only four American ships sailed on this line. Two of them — the S.S. Washington and the S.S. Manhattan — were out of the question for us due to financial considerations. This left only the S.S. Harding and the S.S. Roosevelt. With the S.S. Harding already fully booked, our only alternative was the S.S. Roosevelt, which left Hamburg one day after Yom Tov. So we celebrated our final Pesach in Germany and planned to leave Leipzig on Tuesday night, April 11, upon the conclusion of the holiday.

Since my father was the lone *shochet* remaining in Leipzig at the time, the Jewish community was most grateful that we remained in the city for the holidays. "At least we won't have to have a *milchigen Seder*," one remarked. My father showed his total dedication to the community by slaughtering for one more hour even on Tuesday night, right before we departed for the railroad station. This way, at least some Jews would have chicken for *Shabbos*, he reasoned.

❧ ❧ ❧

On Thursday, March 30, just four days before the beginning of Pesach, which started on the following Monday night, the Nazi authorities suddenly permitted the Broder Shul to reopen. However, the *shul* was in no condition to be used for religious services. The entire interior lay in ruins after the rampages of Kristallnacht. With broken benches and other furnishings piled high on top of each other and religious articles strewn all over the ground, it was an arduous task merely to enter the premises. No one really expected the *shul* to be renovated and made suitable for services in time for Pesach.

Yet somehow it was. More than fifty Jews, some of them professional carpenters, some ordinary laymen, worked feverishly for many hours daily to restore the *shul* to its prior majesty. Even children participated in this renovation project. It was our task to help carry out the debris — and there was plenty of it — from the synagogue grounds.

What a beautiful sight it was, as we entered our *shul* on the first night of Pesach! What a grand feeling! Tears of joy could be seen rolling down the cheeks of many adults. The *shul* had never been so beautiful, I told my mother as we arrived home for the first *Seder*.

My father was not so hasty to display his gratitude to the Nazi regime. He did not rush right out to shower the Nazis with praise and commendations. A kidnapper is not entitled to any expression of thanks when he eventually returns his innocent victims and restores their freedom. His unlawful imprisonment of humans, though only temporary, can never be exonerated. In a similar vein, my father reasoned, the Nazis could never be absolved for their immoral acts of desecrating and destroying Jewish houses of worship on Kristallnacht, and thus depriving law-abiding Jews of their religious rights. These heinous and atrocious crimes would forever be recorded in the annals of Jewish history.

Why did the Nazis permit the Broder Shul to reopen? It was the general feeling among the Jews that it certainly was not a sudden outburst of love and admiration toward Jews which contributed to their actions. It was rather a clever ploy, used to regain some degree of respectability among the nations of the world, which inspired them. Still maintaining their fictional claims that the events of Kristallnacht were due to the spontaneous indignation of the German masses, the authorities felt that the reopening of *shuls* would go a long way in proving to the world that Germany extended religious freedom to all its citizens, and that law and order prevailed at all times.

❧ ❧ ❧

Leaving Leipzig was not the pleasant event I had anticipated for so long. As soon as our day of departure was finalized, a feeling of dejection overcame me. It suddenly dawned upon me that Tante Hinde was remaining in Germany. She had been part of the family for as far back as I could remember. She always cared about us. She possessed so much warmth. She was a most compassionate human being, and there existed a mutual feeling of love between us. And now we were leaving her. We were leaving her alone among the Nazis, to a future of torture and oppression.

Many of our friends came to the *Hauptbahnhof* to bid us farewell, despite the fact that our train left after midnight. The Tetzners came but said their good-byes before we entered the station. They were afraid to be seen among so many Jews in the station, and thus be accused of the "crime" of having Jewish friends.

There were many moving scenes in the station that night, and tears were easily shed. As the train pulled out of the station, perhaps forty or fifty people waved to us from the platform. I can still remember my aunt waving, waving until she disappeared in the distance. We would never see her again.

As soon as we arrived in the United States, an affidavit was sent to my aunt by a distant relative, for her to receive sometime between late May and early July. But it was too late. She became one of the six million martyrs.

When I was in Leipzig in July 1990, I made an attempt to trace her with the help of the *Gemeinde's* lists of Jews deported to concentration camps. Upon completion of the Wannsee Conference, which determined the "final solution to the Jewish problem," mass deportations of Leipzig's Jews began in earnest. On January 21, 1942, Botho Furch, otherwise known as the Eichmann of Leipzig, sent more than seven hundred of Leipzig's Jews to the death camp in Riga, Latvia. The assembly point for this deportation was the gymnasium of the *Hoehere Israelitische Schule*. When I perused this list of names, I found my aunt's name listed, yet for some unknown reason, it was crossed out. I found that a similar situation existed in all future deportations. She was, at first, scheduled for deportation and each time, her name was crossed off the list. She was still alive in Leipzig as late as February 1944, one of the last Jews remaining. There, the *Gemeinde's* records abruptly ended and we could trace her no further.

Before we left Leipzig, four families gave us the names and addresses of their relatives who lived in New York. They had written to them previously, describing the Jews' sorry plight in Hitler's Germany and pleading with them to grant them affidavits which would ultimately enable them to immigrate to the United States. Unfortunately, however, their pleas up to this point had encountered nothing but delay and procrastination. My parents were asked to personally stress to these families the extreme urgency of this matter, and to emphasize that time was of the essence. Jewish lives were at stake.

Upon our arrival in America, my father visited these families and all were overjoyed to receive personal regards from their relatives in Germany. Yet, despite his valiant attempts at persuasion, my father was unable to arouse these people from their apathetic and stolid attitude. They appeared unwilling to assume the financial responsibilities entailed in the issuance of an affidavit.

Perhaps these people felt that my father was exaggerating the dangers confronting German Jewry. Hadn't many other New York Jews often told us that the situation in Germany couldn't really be as critical and hopeless as we portrayed it? It was rather difficult to believe that human beings were capable of such atrocities as those perpetrated by the Nazis. "We'll think about it" and "we'll consider it" was the extent of the commitment of these four families.

My father would often discuss the phlegmatic attitude of these four families and the failure of what he considered a life-saving mission. Had these American families responded in time, the lives of four Jewish families in Leipzig could possibly have been saved. Who knows, my father added, how many more German families had appealed similarly to their brethren in the United States without receiving any kind of reply to their desperate entreaties. Their pleas fell on deaf ears and they perished among the six million *Kedoshim*.

Six

The "Final Solution"

I N THE EARLY 1930's, IN THE PRE-HITLER ERA, Leipzig's Jewish population had reached its peak of 18,000. During the ensuing years, we saw it steadily dwindle due to emigration and deportations carried out en masse. By May 1, 1939, there were only 6,000 Jews remaining in Leipzig.

On May 1, 1939, the policy of *Zwangseinweisung* in *Judenwohnungen* began. Jews were forcibly ousted from their residences and resettled in specific "Jewish houses" west of the Hauptbahnhof. This new Jewish ghetto comprised an area of five streets (Packhoff, Keil, Humboldt, Eberhard, and Parthenstrasse) ranging from the Gerberstrasse to the Walter Bluemel Strasse (now Loehrstrasse). Residences in this area were continually changed, with some families being forced to move as many as seven times a year.

In December 1939, Botho Furch was able to claim that western Leipzig was totally Judenrein, and eventually the north, south, and east followed suit. With all the Jews now concentrated and confined in a tiny area, the authorities would be able to deal with them in a more efficient manner.

Although I was quite familiar with this ghetto area from the 1930's, I carefully scrutinized it this year during my visit. I even entered some houses to better familiarize myself with the space available. I must declare that it still boggles my mind when I attempt to visualize almost six thousand Jews crowded into such a small area.

The outbreak of World War II brought new oppressive regulations upon the Jewish community. Although there was a food shortage throughout Germany in the late 1930's and many items were in short supply, there was at that time no distinction made between Aryans and Jews. Ration cards were issued to all on an equal basis. This changed drastically when the letter "J" began to be stamped on the coupons issued to Jews. From then on, Jews would be permitted to purchase food only in certain designated stores. Many food items were simply not available in these stores. Fruits and vegetables were of inferior quality, as only leftovers from other stores were sold there. Jews were often forced to forego such necessities as milk because only limited amounts of such staples were sent to these establishments.

Many other ordinances, regulations, orders and other decrees were promulgated during the early 1940's to deprive the Jews of every political, civic and economic right. Nazi actions against the Jews were all "legal," and in the days to come, the very act of genocide was in keeping with the new "law" as interpreted by the Gestapo.

The yellow *Judenstern, which Jews were required to wear to show their "identity".*

Leipzig's Jews were required to wear armbands with a *Mogen David*. Later, they were forced to wear a yellow *Judenstern* (Jewish star) with the word *Jude* printed in the center. Several Jews were arrested at this juncture because the Nazis felt that the *Judenstern*, though worn, was not clearly visible to everyone. So the charge in these arrests was "attempting to conceal his Jewish identity."

Jewish drivers' licenses were suspended. No Jew was permitted to have a telephone. Jews owning pianos or radios were required to turn them over to the authorities. Use of public transportation was strictly forbidden, with few exceptions. All residences were to be marked with a *Judenstern*.

The Rosenthal was a beautiful park, easily accessible from all parts of the Jewish section. On an ordinary *Shabbos* afternoon, hundreds of Jews, dressed in their *Shabbos* finery, could be seen leisurely strolling on its paths and availing themselves of its facilities. The *Schwanenteich*, right near the entrance of the park, was a most popular site and many Jewish children frequented it.

This Jewish presence at the park apparently irked the leaders of the Nazi Labor Party (NSDAP). They dispatched a letter to Leipzig's *Oberbuergermeister* stating, "Our beautiful Rosenthal is, for all practical purposes, lost to us. Jews appear to have taken over. Any decent Aryan would find himself most uncomfortable in these surroundings." They suggested that Jews be prohibited from entering the Rosenthal's grounds. The *Oberbuergermeister* complied. Only a minuscule area of the Rosenthal, between Leibniz and Zoellnerweg, remained open to Jews.

Eventually, the Ariowitsch Home for the Elderly was disbanded and the Gestapo occupied the building. The Eitingon *Krankenhaus* was closed and its patients transferred to barracks in Doesen, one of Leipzig's suburbs. This facility was approachable only by crossing a plank, thereby effectively separating it from the adjacent clinic. Two Jewish doctors, who were no longer referred to as doctors but rather as "people who treat the sick," remained with the patients.

Thus, even before the full-scale deportations began, the physical annihilation of the Jews was already in full progress. As a result of hard slave labor, malnutrition, overcrowding, and substandard sanitary conditions, a large number of Jews perished. Due to these prevailing conditions, compounded by the arrests and deportation to concentration camps of numerous individuals, Leipzig's Jewish population shrank to below 3,000 by the end of 1941.

Then the mass deportations began. On January 21, 1942, a total of 715 Jews were deported to the death camp in Riga. Construction of this camp began in July 1941, immediately upon Germany's conquest of Latvia. It was intended to be used in the annihilation of Latvian Jews. To make room for the anticipated arrival of deportees from Germany, more than 30,000 inmates of the camp had been shot in cold blood by the SS just a short time before, in a neighboring forest.

The only available photo of a deportation of Leipzig's Jews, taken circa January 1942.

As the death train stopped in Dresden, an additional three hundred Jews were picked up. The overcrowded train was closely guarded by the SS, and in spite of the cold January weather, no heat was provided. The train's exits were under lock and key to prevent any possible escape. Although the trip to Riga lasted several days, not only was there a severe food shortage on the train, but the traveling Jews also suffered from the lack of drinking water. This was the first, and numerically the largest, deportation of Leipzig's Jews.

The fact that this deportation was prepared and ready to go just one day after the conclusion of the Wannsee Conference was due mainly to the vigorous efforts and superb abilities of Leipzig's own Eichmann, Botho Furch, who was completely committed and devoted to this work. In a letter to Leipzig's *Oberbuergermeister* dated July 14, 1942, in which Furch mentions his connections to the Gestapo, he discusses the urgency of immediate transports of Jews to Theresienstadt. In this manner, buildings in the Leipzig ghetto near the *Hauptbahnhof* would become available.

Other deportations followed. On May 10, 1943, a group of 369 Jews was sent to the death camp in Belzyce, Poland, near the city of Lublin. Three of these deportees, one man and two women, were killed immediately upon their arrival at the camp.

On July 13, 1942, a transport of 170 to 191 Jews was sent *nach Osten* (to the east). It has now been clearly established that the destination of this transport was Trostinez, near Minsk, where upon their arrival a mass execution was carried out by the SS. Although Nazi documents used the word "resettlement" in describing the purpose of this deportation *nach Osten*, one must realize that in the language of the Nazis, "resettlement" was synonymous with "execution." The same holds true of the deportations for "resettlement" in Theresienstadt, since Theresienstadt was only a temporary stopover and the deportees would eventually be sent *nach Osten*. With few exceptions, nothing was ever heard again from any of these deportees. They became part of the six million martyrs.

Between September 11 and September 19, 443 to 476 Jews were deported to Theresienstadt. On February 17, 1943, a group of 184 was deported *nach Osten*. With the shrinking Jewish population, fewer Jews were left for future deportations. On June 18, 1943, 23 Jews were sent to Theresienstadt, and on January 13, 1944, another 33 were sent to the same destination. Additional transports were sent to Auschwitz, Buchenwald, Dachau, and several other camps.

When the final transport of 169 Jews left Leipzig on February 14, 1945, heading in the direction of Theresienstadt, it seemed that the "final solution of the Jewish problem" had been reached in Leipzig, at least. Leipzig had become *Judenrein*.

Fortunately, the Soviet army captured Theresienstadt soon thereafter and liberated most of the deportees in the final transport. They were now able to return to Leipzig if they so desired.

Seven

After the War

N 1935, APPROXIMATELY 18,000 JEWS lived in Leipzig. Approximately 4,000 — mainly those who emigrated in time — were able to survive. Few survived the concentration camps, although some survivors did return to Leipzig after the war. In May and June, 1945, the *Israelitische Religionsgemeinde zu Leipzig* was organized once again.

Restoration of the Broder Shul became a prime task for the newly established *Gemeinde*. The Nazis had occupied the building during the war and had turned it into a storage house for chemicals. With the defeat of Nazism an accomplished fact, the building was returned to Jewish hands, who immediately proceeded to renovate and refurbish the sanctuary. On Sunday, October 28, 1945, the *shul* was finally rededicated in a festive ceremony. Survivors from the concentration camps comprised the audience.

By the end of 1945, Leipzig's Jewish population had increased to almost 300. Approximately half of them were returning Leipzigers, former members of the *Gemeinde*. Since few returnees were from the younger generations, though, the population has naturally declined. Today, the *Gemeinde* has only 36 members. Its chairman is Herr Aron Adlerstein, a survivor of Auschwitz, one of the last *Ostjuden* to settle in Leipzig after the war.

Of those Leipzigers who had been deported to Auschwitz, Frau Ella Wittman was the lone survivor. When she returned to Leipzig after the war, she found it extremely difficult to relate any of her experiences at Auschwitz; it was too painful for her.

We met Frau Wittman at the *Religionsgemeinde* in August 1980, where she was performing secretarial functions. She was eighty-one years old at the time. She graciously invited us to her home on the Gustav Adolf Strasse, and we accepted the invitation.

Soon we discovered that Frau Wittman was all alone in the world. Every member of her family had been murdered by the Nazis, and she did not have a single relative anywhere. She would love to leave East Germany, she told us, but then she would no longer be eligible for old-age pensions. Having no other income, she had no choice but to remain in Leipzig.

I asked her how she got along with her Christian neighbors, and her answer was most revealing. She recognizes many of her present, supposedly friendly, neighbors as the very same people who, during the Hitler era, made life miserable for her and her family. She is convinced that a large number of Germans remain, even today, vicious anti-Semites. Today, however, it has become fashionable for Germans to display tolerance toward Jews. It is part of the new public image they are trying to project. So, in public at least, the Germans follow this new vogue religiously. In their hearts, however, Frau Wittman was convinced that she was still considered a pariah, an outcast, in her neighborhood.

As a result, concluded Frau Wittman, a relationship between the Christians and herself was virtually nonexistent. Greetings of *"Guten Tag"* and *"Auf Wiedersehen"* are the extent of their relationship.

A completely different response was given to me by Herr Eugen Gollomb, who in 1967 became the *Vorsitzende* of the Jewish *Gemeinde*. "One must realize that all Nazis now reside in West Germany," he explained. "There are no ex-Nazis living in our midst."

It was difficult for me to believe that Herr Gollomb himself actually believed this Communist line. Late in 1989, the East Germans officially accepted their share of the blame for the Holocaust. Their citizens too were guilty, they finally admitted.

A Personal Glimpse into Modern Germany

MY OWN OBSERVATIONS DURING MY THREE TRIPS to Germany, two of which brought me to Leipzig, fully substantiate Frau Wittman's contention concerning anti-Semitism in Germany today. Many a German has expressed to me his deep regret and anguish about what his countrymen perpetrated upon the Jews. How could we have committed such horrendous crimes against human beings? they question. How could one Hitler have misled so many decent Germans?

In Leipzig, several monuments have been erected to express contempt for Nazi terror. *Gedenkt! Vergesst es nicht!* (Remember! Don't forget!) proclaims the monument at the site of the destroyed *Gemeinde* synagogue at the Gottschedstrasse. Monuments with similar expressions can be found at the Carlebach Schule, at the lone area of the Rosenthal which remained open to Jews, and at the new Jewish cemetery at Eutritzsch. On the Parthenstrasse, where during the pogrom of November 10, 1938 Jews had been thrown into a stream, the monument reads, "Where is your brother?"

However, despite these outward displays of solidarity and friendship, occasionally a completely different picture emerges. It is a picture of enmity and animosity directed toward the stubborn Jews, who simply refuse to disappear from the face of the earth. Let me cite some cases in point.

As we entered Germany from Basel, Switzerland, and stopped at the bank to obtain some German currency, I overheard one woman telling another, "The Jews, they're back, and you thought we'd gotten rid of them forever." I overheard a similar comment in Leipzig's Am Ring Hotel this past July. At the same bank, when I asked a teller about the currency rates, I was abruptly told, "You Jews have always been stingy and money crazy. No wonder no one likes you."

A saleswoman at the Munich airport completely ignored my presence in the store when I entered to purchase a newspaper. When I insisted on service, I was curtly told, "It's about time you people realized that you're not wanted in this country. This is Deutschland — not Judenland." She then reluctantly sold me the newspaper.

When I entered a parking lot ahead of a German who was convinced that he saw the empty spot before I did, I was greeted with "Verfluchter Jude! Dreckischer Jude!" and several other familiar epithets from the Nazi era. I still don't know how he knew that I was a Jew.

While standing in line at the checkout counter of a tiny fruit store, a German physically attempted to push me aside, and when he failed to do so, his advice to me was "Jude, why don't you go to Palestine to kill some Arabs?" When I chose to ignore his outburst, he ordered, "Jude, raus von Deutschland." (Jew, get out of Germany.) My continued silence angered him into yet further anti-Semitic comments.

Monument at the New Cemetary.

GEDENKT

IN DER
STADT LEIPZIG
FIELEN 14000
BÜRGER
JÜDISCHEN
GLAUBENS DEM
FASCHISTISCHEN
TERROR
ZUM OPFER

HIER WURDE AM
9, NOVEMBER 1938
DIE GROSSE SYNAGOGE
DER ISRAELITISCHEN
RELIGIONSGEMEINDE
ZU LEIPZIG DURCH
BRANDSTIFTUNG
FASCHISTISCHER
HORDEN ZERSTÖRT

VERGESST ES NICHT

Monument at the Gemeinde Synagogue.   Plaque at the Hoehere Israelitische Schule.

A woman in a motel was visibly angry at me when I dared to correct a mistake in my bill which she had computed. I then distinctly heard her whispering that some people are like mosquitoes. When I asked her for an explanation of this deep philosophical thought, she consented to explain it to me. Although G-d has given life to the mosquito, humans are nevertheless permitted to kill it because a mosquito is detrimental to life. Likewise, she reasoned, it is permissible to kill humans who are detrimental to life. She refused to commit herself as to which humans she was referring to; yet the implication seems quite clear.

When I asked a young female police officer in Frankfurt whether she could perhaps permit me to remain in the no-parking zone for one or two minutes while I waited for my sister to return to the car, I was immediately informed that this is not New York. "There are laws in Germany, and Jews cannot simply come and break them at their whim and fancy as they did in the past."

Not everyone, however, was able to recognize me as a Jew. When a young lady inquired as to where I was from and I mentioned the city of New York, she expressed her fond wish to visit New York some day. She then added that she had absolutely no desire to reside there on a permanent basis, though, because "there are too many Jews living in New York, and you know what they're like." She was obviously stunned when I revealed to her that I was one of those New York Jews. She became quite apologetic and insisted that she was not referring to me. However, I was convinced that her low opinion of Jews must be attributed to the anti-Semitic propaganda to which she has been exposed. Since she had never even talked to a Jew, I could not really fault her for her biased opinion. She readily agreed with my conclusion and added that she hears many derogatory and debasing comments about Jews from her parents and friends.

❦ ❦ ❦

In April 1971, two short notices appeared in the *Jewish Chronicle*. Fourteen gravestones were overturned and damaged in the ancient Jewish cemetery at Hochberg, in the Ludwigsburg district. Swastikas were scratched on all twelve glass doors of the historic Paulus Church in Frankfurt, where an exhibition on the theme of Anti-Fascist Resistance 1933-1945 was being held. Many other such incidents have been noted in the press. It is worthwhile to point out that there are synagogues in Germany today which require armed police to protect them from the virulent and venomous anti-Semitism so rife and prevalent among the present German population. There are still many "former" Nazis running businesses and local government administrations who have not forgotten the glorious days of the Third Reich and yearn for their return. So much for those who claim that anti-Semitism has all but disappeared in Germany.

Such is the state of tolerance toward Jews in Germany today. Although the general climate is not anti-Semitic and anti-Semitism no longer predominates, its ugly head can often be seen lurking in the shadows. Yes, Frau Wittman's assessment was absolutely correct. They still do not like us in Germany. We are still considered an inferior people, unworthy of treading upon German soil.

Although anti-Semitism also exists in the United States, it exists to a much lesser degree. In all of my fifty-one years in the United States, I had not experienced as many anti-Semitic encounters as I did in a week in Germany.

At Berlin's Tegel Airport, a young German was discussing his misgivings about the forthcoming reunification of Germany. The basic German philosophy of *Deutschland ueber Alles*, as incorporated in the German national anthem, remains unaltered today, he explained. It loudly proclaims, "We are the master race; we are superior to all else." Such prevailing concepts and fundamental beliefs can easily serve as the base from which a renewed wave of anti-Semitism can suddenly emerge. Jews could again become the scapegoats for all failures and shortcomings of the newly-formed Fourth Reich.

This scenario of future events appears, at first glance, to be incredible indeed. However, many authorities, closely familiar with the German national character, have emphatically warned us that such a tragic future is well within the realm of possibility. It is therefore quite disturbing to see so many Jews returning to settle in Germany today.

There are more neo-Nazis operating in the territory of the former East Germany than in the former West Germany, according to Peter Frisch, a senior official of the *Verfassungsschutz*, Germany's FBI. In an interview published in the *Flensburger Tageblatt*, Frisch was quoted as saying that the authorities had trouble keeping track of right-wing extremist groups in the former East Germany, where the existence of neo-Nazi organizations had been all but denied by the deposed Communist regime. As recently as October 1990, hundreds of neo-Nazi demonstrators marched through Dresden, in the former East Germany, shouting racist slogans. In Leipzig, neo-Nazi violence led to the police shooting of one person, who eventually died.

Heinz Galinski, head of Germany's Jewish community, has called on government leaders to address the problem before it gets completely out of hand. The Auschwitz survivor said that since unification, hardly a day goes by that Jews are not attacked somewhere in Germany. Anti-Semitism is alive and well in Deutschland.

Despite the numerous calls by Jewish leaders and Holocaust survivors for an anti-Nazi clause to be included in the country's new constitution, perhaps to ban Nazi groups completely, no action has, as yet, been taken by the unified German government. It should be noted that a long-standing Allied ban on neo-Nazi groups in Berlin was recently lifted as wartime allies forfeited control over the city.

The renowned American writer, William Shirer, who authored the best-seller, *The Rise and Fall of the Third Reich*, resided in Germany for many years. As an American reporter in pre-World War II Germany, he was quite familiar with the country and the philosophy of its citizens. In a recent interview in the *New York*

Times, he expressed his deep anxieties and apprehensions concerning German reunification. He had many friends among the German liberals and socialists before the war, but when Hitler gained power, they became active Nazis. During Kristallnacht, he encountered these very same friends looting and plundering Jewish establishments. The Germans cannot be trusted, concludes Shirer.

Approximately one month after the reunification of Germany, the following item appeared in the *New York Times*. In September 1990, two soccer matches in Berlin and one in Leipzig led to regular street battles between rival fans and the police. At a match between Leipzig and Football Club Jena, fighting in the stands caused officials to cut play short. Neo-Nazi groups are often at the core of the fighting, and in some stadiums, groups of violent youths have taken to jeering referees by chanting, "Jew!" Apparently no greater insult can be hurled at a member of the so-called "master race," even after reunification.

☙ ☙ ☙

During my first return to Leipzig in August 1980, I sat motionless near the hotel window and looked out to the street below. I remembered the thousands of Leipzig's Jews who, in the past, had created an atmosphere of warmth and friendship in the city. I remembered the warmth of my home in the heart of Jewish Leipzig. I remembered my classmates who, despite the Nazi terror, helped to make my early childhood a happy one. I remembered the throngs of peace-loving Jews, leisurely strolling in the Rosenthal on *Shabbos* afternoon. I remembered the beautiful *Yamim Tovim* and the sense of friendship and togetherness we experienced on those joyous occasions. I even remembered the beauty and warmth of the old buildings which served as residences for Leipzig's Jews.

All of this had vanished. The streets were now devoid of anything Jewish. The city had lost its warmth and the stones of the now dilapidated and decayed houses projected a most frigid atmosphere. Gone are the Jews and everything else I ever treasured in the city of my birth. The city had become to me a city of strangers. For more than two hours I sat by the open window absorbed in these thoughts, with tears rolling down my cheeks. It was truly a sad and disheartening experience for me.

The following morning I approached an elderly woman at the post office and asked her whether the street we were on, now called the Karl Marx Platz, wasn't once known as the Augustus Platz. "So you remember," she said with a feeling of surprise. "Wasn't Leipzig much nicer then? So we got rid of the Jews and turned a warm and friendly city into a city of ice." Exactly my feelings, I thought. I was not quite sure whether the woman recognized me as a Jew.

All these events have delivered a powerful message to me. Any Jewish city anywhere could potentially suffer Leipzig's fate, *chas v'shalom*. There is no safety and security for us in *galus*, even in a democracy. The German Weimar Republic was a democracy, yet it could not prevent the emergence of a Hitler. When the anti-Semites so decreed, Leipzig, a city of 18,000 Jews, became *Judenrein*.

The Talmud teaches: עַל מִי יֵשׁ לָנוּ לְהִשָּׁעֵן? עַל אָבִינוּ שֶׁבַּשָּׁמַיִם. — "Our only salvation is in the hands of our Father in Heaven" (*Sotah* 49a).

In his eulogy of the late Ponevezer *Rav*, HaGaon HaRav Yosef Shlomo Kahaneman (printed in the *Sefer Zichron Shmuel*) the *Gaon* HaRav Shmuel Rozovsky, the former *Rosh HaYeshivah* of the Ponevezer Yeshivah in Bnei Brak, quoted HaRav Kahaneman as saying that he believed and continuously declared publicly that this present generation which survived the Holocaust, would be the generation which will witness the Redemption from *galus*. I was privileged to be personally present when HaRav Kahaneman expressed this view to my distinguished *Rebbe*, HaGaon HaRav Eliezer Silver during one of his frequent visits to HaRav Silver's home in Cincinnati. I can still recall that HaRav Silver wholeheart-edly supported this view. A similar view has often been expressed by the renowned Lubavitcher *Rebbe*, HaRav Menachem Schneer-son, and by many other Rabbinic authorities.

We hope and pray that the view of these *gedolim* will soon be confirmed and that *Hashem* will redeem us from the dreadful ordeal of *galus* with the coming of the *Mashiach* speedily in our days.

Epilogue

Explaining the Holocaust

"Rabbi — רַבִּי שִׁמְעוֹן בַּר יוֹחָאִי אוֹמֵר, הֲלָכָה בְּיָדוּעַ שֶׁעֵשָׂו שׂוֹנֵא לְיַעֲקֹב
Shimon bar Yochai taught: It is a known *halachah* that Esau hates
Jacob" (*Sifri, Beha'alosecha*, chapter 24). Many commentaries have
questioned the term *halachah* as used in this context. *Halachah* is
a generic term for the entire legal system of Judaism, embracing all
the detailed laws and observances. *Halachah* mandates guidelines
to the Jews. It teaches a system of conduct to adhere to. The fact
that Esau hates Jacob is, therefore, not in the realm of *halachah*,
but it is rather of a sociological nature, one dealing with social
relationships and patterns of collective behavior. The term
halachah, therefore, appears to be a misnomer.

The great Warsaw *Gaon*, Rabbi Menachem Ziemba, in his book *Chidushei HaGarmaz* (chapter 48), offers a solution to our problem. Let me now attempt to elaborate on it.

Rabbi Chanina ben Dosa teaches: כָּל שֶׁמַּעֲשָׂיו מְרוּבִּין מֵחָכְמָתוֹ, חָכְמָתוֹ מִתְקַיֶּימֶת; וְכָל שֶׁחָכְמָתוֹ מְרוּבָה מִמַּעֲשָׂיו אֵין חָכְמָתוֹ מִתְקַיֶּימֶת — "Anyone whose deeds exceed his wisdom, his wisdom shall endure; but anyone whose wisdom exceeds his deeds, his wisdom shall not endure" (*Avos* 3:12). The question often raised is since a person can act only within the scope of his knowledge and intelligence, how can one's deeds ever exceed one's wisdom?

The Torah informs us that when *Hashem* offered the Torah to the Jewish people, they unanimously replied: נַעֲשֶׂה וְנִשְׁמָע, "All that *Hashem* has said we shall do and understand." By placing action prior to comprehension, the Israelites removed their right to selection and discretion. Their faith in *Hashem* was so abundant that they consented to follow His directions blindly, irrespective of their significance and meaning.

This unqualified preparedness to do even that which they did not comprehend was tantamount to performing beyond their knowledge. Hence, their deeds, in the form of their readiness, exceeded their wisdom.

Rabban Gamliel, the son of Rabbi Yehudah *HaNasi*, suggests that this then be the blueprint and guideline to all adherents of the Jewish faith. His instructions are as explicit as they are unqualified. בַּטֵּל רְצוֹנְךָ מִפְּנֵי רְצוֹנוֹ, "Negate your own will before the will of the Almighty" (*Avos* 2:4).

When one discovers that his own will clashes with the views and directives of the Torah, he ought to undo his will and submit to the will of the Torah. Whether or not one can rationally perceive the wisdom of what he is commanded to do, and even when his will clearly and insistently urges him to head in another direction, Rabban Gamliel still recommends that we subject ourselves to the higher authority of Heaven.

The Torah must be looked upon as a binding ordinance and not merely as a menu from which one sporadically chooses and picks up items of interest to suit his craving and fancy.

Ultimately, the test of true faith is its ability to go beyond the rational, the reasonable, the understood, and to move man to deeds though they run counter to his will. That is indeed religion in its highest form.

Despite this, many attempts have been made to obtain rational explanations for our Torah laws. Reasons given for the *dinei kashrus*, our dietary laws, are an example. Many have suggested preventive medicine as the logical elucidation for our laws of *kashrus*, and facts seem to bear this out.

Few observant Jews have ever been afflicted with the dread disease trichinosis, which supposedly is a direct result of eating contaminated pork, or with a certain type of hepatitis, which results from consumption of contaminated oysters. Jews have apparently been protected by the dietary laws from the common and dangerous illness tularemia, a sickness transmitted mostly by the hare or hyrax of the rabbit family. Jews abstain from crab and lobster, which are known to be ptomaine generators. The removal of hard fat from each animal has been lauded by medical science in its struggle to keep man's appetite away from saturated fats. A foremost authority on heart disease, Dr. Paul Dudley White, advised the American Medical Association to pay careful heed to the Biblical command, כָּל חֵלֶב שׁוֹר וְכֶשֶׂב וָעֵז לֹא תֹאכֵלוּ, "Every manner of fat you shall not eat" (*Vayikra* 7:23).

Tuberculosis, pleurisy, or other respiratory diseases in an animal render it unkosher. As a matter of fact, many modern United States government regulations are, in essence, no less than a tacit acceptance and general adaptation of the kosher meat inspection rules of Judaism.

But can anyone actually assert with any reasonable measure of certainty that preventive medicine is the reason behind our dietary laws? A hog could be raised in an incubator on antibiotics, bathed daily, slaughtered in a hospital operating room, and its carcass sterilized by ultraviolet rays, without rendering its meat kosher. To dramatize this point, Rabbi Elazar ben Azarya taught: אַל יֹאמַר אָדָם אִי אֶפְשִׁי לֶאֱכוֹל בְּשַׂר חֲזִיר אֲבָל אֶפְשִׁי וּמָה אֶעֱשֶׂה וְאָבִי שֶׁבַּשָּׁמַיִם גָּזַר עָלַי כָּךְ — "A person should not say, 'I loathe swine's flesh.' He should rather say, 'I do desire it, but what could I do, my Father in Heaven has decreed against it'" (Toras Kohanim, Vayikra 20:26).

The Torah rarely discloses reasons for its statutes. This may be due to the limited aptitude of our minds in relation to the depth of the subject. Furthermore, once a reason is revealed, people may rationalize the statutes out of existence by searching for situations where the reason does not apply. In the two statutes for which the Torah did disclose reasons, even Shlomo HaMelech rationalized and stumbled (Sanhedrin 21b).

This, however, does not prevent our learned scholars from advancing reasons which expound and explicate various statutes of our Torah. We can, however, under no circumstances be certain as to their validity and accuracy. Hence, all our conclusions and inferences derived from these explications are inconclusive. Perhaps the rapid advance of modern science and technology will eventually rebut and refute these reasons entirely. Yet the Torah is eternal, and its statutes remain intact regardless of the authenticity of the reasons advanced.

Even if pork were the most wholesome and nutritious food on the market, we may not partake of it. We abstain from it solely because of Hashem's directive. Our faith in Him should be so unswerving that we would forsake the directives of our own intelligence and follow His directives blindly.

❦ ❦ ❦

Rabbi Menachem Ziemba contends that a similar situation exists concerning the sociological fact that Esau (the nations of the world) hates Jacob (the Jewish nation). Many reasons have been submitted throughout the ages for the causes of anti-Semitism, yet the causes often appear contradictory in nature and are totally inconsistent. In one country the Jews are despised because they are capitalists; in another country the Jews are hated because they are socialists. Here they are scorned because of their superior intelligence, and there they are detested because, due to their inadequacies, they constantly present a burden upon the community. Some abhor Jews because of their extreme religiosity, and others loathe them because they are spreading doctrines contrary to Christian dogma.

Early German Jewish leaders proclaimed a policy of "be a Jew at home and a German away from home." They assured us that this would be the panacea that would end anti-Semitism for all time. Yet this policy did not prevent the rise of Nazism.

Rabbi Shimon bar Yochai suggests that anti-Semitism is in the same category as *halachah*. We know of no specific reason for it. It is a blind hatred, and all of Jacob's attempts at appeasement will prove to be ineffective. Some methods may even be counterproductive and increase hatred, as Esau deeply resents Jacob's attempt to climb to his brother's lofty status in society.

What solution does Rabbi Ziemba offer to assure our survival in a world steeped in anti-Semitism? In chapter 49 of his book, he quotes the verse וַיְמָרְרוּ אֶת חַיֵּיהֶם בַּעֲבֹדָה קָשָׁה בְּחֹמֶר וּבִלְבֵנִים, "The Egyptians embittered the life of the Israelites with hard work with mortar and with bricks" (*Shemos* 1:14). Upon this verse, the *Zohar* comments: The word חֹמֶר refers to the system of a fortiori, which is one of the thirteen methods we have at our disposal to derive statutes pertaining to Torah, and the word לְבֵנִים refers to the clarification of *halachah*. Through the process of Torah study, concludes Rabbi Ziemba, we gain the spiritual strength and power to withstand the pain and agony of oppression (as symbolized by mortar and bricks) perpetrated upon us during our years in *galus*.

David HaMelech taught: אֵלֶּה בָרֶכֶב וְאֵלֶּה בַסּוּסִים וַאֲנַחְנוּ בְּשֵׁם ה' אֱלֹקֵינוּ נַזְכִּיר, "Some of our foes rely on chariots and others on cavalry, but we trust in *Hashem*" (*Tehillim* 20:8). *Hashem* and our Torah are our shields and our keys for survival.

❀ ❀ ❀

One of the most troubling theological questions of our time is, why did *Hashem* see fit to bring the Holocaust upon the Jews? How should a tragedy of such awesome proportions be viewed from a Torah perspective? The world-renowned *Gaon*, Rabbi Aharon Soloveichik, has shed much light on the subject, and I am most grateful to Arie Marcus, one of the *Gaon's* disciples, for excerpting his views.

After *Hashem* forgave the Israelites for making the golden calf, Moshe asked *Hashem*, הַרְאֵנִי נָא אֶת כְּבוֹדֶךָ, "Please reveal Your glory to me." *Hashem* responded, וְרָאִיתָ אֶת אֲחוֹרָי וּפָנַי לֹא יֵרָאוּ, "You shall see My back, but My face shall not be seen" (*Shemos* 33:18,23). The *Midrash* explains that *Hashem* was telling Moshe that a person, as part of this world (*lefanai*) cannot fully comprehend events which are intellectually perplexing and emotionally troubling. Only after this world and its history will have been completed (*achorai*) will the enigma of *Hashem's* will be fully understood.

Rabbi Soloveichik then illustrated the message of this *Midrash* with the following incident. He was once invited to the home of an art connoisseur who showed him his collection of paintings. As he approached one of the works to get a closer look, his host said, "Rabbi, you can't appreciate the painting unless you are at a distance of five feet." If one cannot appreciate the painting of a human artist unless it is viewed from a distance, certainly the master plan of *Hashem* cannot be adequately perceived or comprehended until it reaches completion in the end of days. Only when *Hashem* will have filled the canvas of history with the tempera of time can one begin to realize the rationale for what has transpired.

When one attempts, in our times, to find meaning in the Holocaust, he is, in essence, trying to appreciate a complex painting from a distance of two inches. He is actually attempting something that Moshe *Rabbeinu* himself was told he could not do. For *Hashem* had told him that His works could be viewed only in retrospect, from afar, at a distance of space and time.

It is evident from this discussion that the Torah's teaching should make us recognize our limitations. Inasmuch as we are part of history, and especially since we are so close to the events, the significance and motivation for the Holocaust remains beyond the grasp of our intellect. To attempt to offer any explanations as to the causes and as to why *Hashem* permitted it to happen, said Rabbi Soloveitchik, involves *gassus haruach*, a sense of arrogance, in that such an attempt assumes knowledge of the master plan of *Hashem*.

❊ ❊ ❊

While according to *halachah* one may not attempt to explain the Holocaust — the way of *Hashem* being hidden from us — the *halachah* does demand action as a response. What should our response be? Maimonides teaches: וְדָבָר זֶה מִדַּרְכֵי הַתְּשׁוּבָה הוּא שֶׁבִּזְמַן שֶׁתָּבֹא צָרָה וְיִזְעֲקוּ עָלֶיהָ וְיָרִיעוּ, יֵדְעוּ הַכֹּל שֶׁבִּגְלַל מַעֲשֵׂיהֶם הָרָעִים הוּרַע לָהֶם וְזֶה הוּא שֶׁיִּגְרוֹם לְהָסִיר הַצָּרָה מֵעֲלֵיהֶם. אֲבָל אִם לֹא יִזְעֲקוּ וְלֹא יָרִיעוּ אֶלָּא יֹאמְרוּ דָּבָר מִמִּנְהַג הָעוֹלָם אֵירַע לָנוּ וְצָרָה זוּ נִקְרֵה נִקְרֵית הָרֵי זוּ דֶּרֶךְ אַכְזָרִיּוּת וְגוֹרֶמֶת הָהֶם להִדָּבֵק בְּמַעֲשֵׂיהֶם הָרָעִים --- "When a tragedy occurs, one must not pass it off as the way of the world, but rather we must assume that it was due to sins. Consequently, it should become a stimulus to repentance. We must search our deeds and correct our shortcomings."

However, it must be emphasized that, although we must attribute tragedy to sin, we dare not point an accusing finger at anyone but ourselves. *Pirkei Avos* teaches that on the public level, there is an obligation of הֱוֵי דָן אֶת כָּל הָאָדָם לְכַף זְכוּת, "One must judge *Klal Yisrael* as a whole only in a favorable manner." There is no license to impute transgressions to the Jewish people nor to blame them for what happened.

Similarly, the great *gaon* Rabbi Yitzchok Hutner, *Rosh HaYeshivah* of Mesifta Rabbi Chaim Berlin, is quoted in the Jewish Observer of October 1977 as saying that we have no right to interpret the events of the *churban* of European Jewry as any kind of punishment for specific sins. One would have to be a prophet or a Talmudic sage to claim knowledge of the specific reasons for what befell us. Anyone on a lesser plane who claims to do so tramples in vain upon the bodies of the *kedoshim* who died *al kiddush Hashem* and misuses the power to interpret and understand Jewish history.

When *Hagaon* Rabbi Eliezer Silver of Cincinnati was asked to explain the meaning of the Holocaust, he simply replied, נִסְתָּרִים דַּרְכֵי הַשֵּׁם, "the ways of *Hashem* are concealed from us." However, he utterly condemned any attempt to point an accusing finger and to place responsibility of this catastrophe squarely on anyone's shoulder.

When the *Navi* Yeshayahu downgraded the Jewish people by declaring, וּבְתוֹךְ עַם טְמֵא שְׂפָתַיִם אָנֹכִי, "I dwell in the midst of a people of unclean lips," it was considered a most grievous sin which required atonement and vindication (*Isaiah* 6:5-7).

Rashi comments that the severity of Yeshayau's sin was due to the fact that there was no Divine command (in the form of a prophecy) which charged Yeshayahu to decry the Jews; nor was this an attempt to admonish them for the purpose of improving their spiritual comport. It was rather an accusatory statement against his fellow Jews made of Yeshayahu's own volition (*Yevamos* 49b).

No Jewish leader, continued HaRav Silver, is granted license to downgrade his own people. To debase the religious character of the Holocaust's victim's by suggesting that their destruction was an inevitable result of specific sins they committed, is not only an unproven theory, but it is quite cruel. How dare one tarnish the memory of the six million *kedoshim* in such a treacherous manner, concluded *HaRav* Silver.

Unfortunately, many people who attempt to explain the Holocaust from a theological perspective do point a finger at the victims, implying or even claiming outright that they were sinners and, therefore, brought the Holocaust upon themselves.

A visiting rabbi to our *beis medrash*, one who had spent the Holocaust years in the safety of America, publicly lectured that the lack of proper decorum observed by European Jewry during synagogue services was the direct cause of the Holocaust.

As I watched the faces of the many concentration camp survivors in the audience, the lecture appeared to me to be both cruel and outright mean-spirited. Rather than display compassion and sympathy, the rabbi blasted the victims and their parents who had perished *al kiddush Hashem* with an unproven theory that is totally groundless.

The results of this lecture became evident immediately upon its completion. One gentleman, with tears coursing down his face, strongly challenged the speaker's hypothesis. His father had been a great *tzaddik* who had always observed proper decorum in the synagogue. Why was he tortured and murdered? Furthermore, he added, were American Jews really more virtuous and noble than their European brothers? Was their synagogue decorum really irreproachable? Other voices of survivors joined the debate, which by now had become an intense confrontation between the self-righteous speaker and the victims, whose religious conduct he had criticized.

Needless to say, the lecture was totally counterproductive. Its only result was to arouse anger and animosity among Torah-observant Jews. If the speaker had sincerely intended to improve decorum within the synagogue, which certainly is a worthwhile goal, he could have achieved success without invoking the pains of the Holocaust and thereby bring distress and agony to so many.

Many of the *gedolim* of our time have expressed similar sentiments to me.

The eminent and renowned *Gaon* from Dvinsk, Rabbi Meir Simchah HaCohen, writes, in his *sefer Meshech Chochmah:* כַּאֲשֶׁר יִשְׂרָאֵל יָשׁוּב לוֹמַר 'אַךְ שֶׁקֶר נָחֲלוּ אֲבוֹתֵינוּ' וּבִכְלַל יִשְׁכַּח מַחֲצַבְתּוֹ וְיֶחֱשֵׁב לְאֶזְרָח רַעֲנָן, יַעֲזוֹב לִימוּדֵי דָתוֹ לִלְמוֹד לְשׁוֹנוֹת לֹא לוֹ, יָלִיף מִקַּלְקָלְתָּא וְלֹא יָלִיף מְתַקַּנְתָּא, יַחֲשׁוֹב כִּי בֶּרְלִין הִיא יְרוּשָׁלַיִם, וְכִמְקוּלְקָלִים שֶׁבָּהֶם עֲשִׂיתֶם כִּמְתוּקָנִים לֹא עֲשִׂיתֶם וְאַל תִּשְׂמַח יִשְׂרָאֵל אֶל גִּיל כָּעֲמִים, אַל יָבֹא רוּחַ סוֹעָר וְסָעַר, יַעֲקוֹר אוֹתוֹ מִגִּזְעוֹ וכו'.

He predicts that destruction will come upon the Jewish people due to their abandonment of Jewish values and slavish adulation of secular culture, as evidenced in the Reform movement in Berlin.

It must be remembered, however, that Rabbi Meir Simchah lived in the years prior to the Holocaust. His book, *Meshech Chochmah*, was published in 1927, six years before Hitler's rise to power. Therefore, he certainly was not pointing an accusing finger at any victims of the Holocaust by theologically rationalizing such an incomprehensible tragedy.

Rabbi Meir Simchah was merely offering a logical and historical explanation as to why such a tragedy might well occur in the future, and in so doing, he was expressing Torah views. The Torah itself is replete with admonitions of potential tragedy if we fail to hearken to the words of *Hashem*. Such calamities are specifically enumerated, and in great detail, in the two *tochachos* found in the Torah. The concept of שָׂכָר וָעוֹנֶשׁ (reward and punishment) is listed among the י"ג עִיקָרִים, the thirteen articles of the Jewish faith.

Biblical texts often discuss the concept of *hester panim* (the hiding of *Hashem's* countenance from those who suffer) when transgressions are committed. וְקָם הָעָם הַזֶּה וְזָנָה אַחֲרֵי אֱלֹהֵי נֵכַר הָאָרֶץ ... וַעֲזָבַנִי וְהֵפֵר אֶת בְּרִיתִי אֲשֶׁר כָּרַתִּי אִתּוֹ. וְחָרָה אַפִּי בוֹ בַיּוֹם הַהוּא וַעֲזַבְתִּים. וְהִסְתַּרְתִּי פָנַי מֵהֶם וְהָיָה לֶאֱכוֹל. וּמְצָאָהוּ רָעוֹת רַבּוֹת וְצָרוֹת וְאָמַר בַּיּוֹם הַהוּא הֲלֹא עַל כִּי אֵין אֱלֹקַי בְּקִרְבִּי מְצָאוּנִי הָרָעוֹת הָאֵלֶּה — "And this people will rise up and go astray after the foreign gods of the land . . . and will forsake Me and break My covenant which I have made with them. Then My anger shall be kindled against them on that day and I will forsake them. And I will hide My face from them and they shall be devoured; and there shall come upon them many evils and troubles; so that they will say on that day: Is it not because our G-d is not among us, that these evils have come upon us?" (*Devarim* 31:16-17).

In a similar vein, Ezra *HaSofer* writes:

הֲנָשׁוּב לְהָפֵר מִצְוֹתֶיךָ וּלְהִתְחַתֵּן בְּעַמֵּי הַתּוֹעֵבוֹת הָאֵלֶּה. הֲלֹא תֶאֱנַף בָּנוּ עַד כַּלֵּה לְאֵין שְׁאֵרִית וּפְלֵיטָה — "Shall we again violate Your commandments and marry with these abominable people? If we do, You will become angry with us to bring upon us total destruction, leaving no remnant and refuge" (*Ezra* 9:14). Many other such forewarnings of impending disaster can be found in our holy Scriptures. This was the true intent of Rabbi Meir Simchah's admonition concerning future destruction.

In conclusion, says Rabbi Aharon Soloveichik, from the *halachic* perspective, there is no adequate explanation any mortal can offer with any amount of certainty for the sins which caused the Holocaust. The ways of the Almighty are hidden from us. Therefore, the approach of ascribing and imputing transgressions to those martyrs who died *al kiddush Hashem* is totally inconsistent with the Torah viewpoint.

However, one dare not attribute the tragic events of such enormity merely to chance, to historical inevitability. Our sages taught us long ago: אֵין אָדָם נוֹקֵף אֶצְבָּעוֹ מִלְמַטָּה אֶלָּא אִם כֵּן מַכְרִיזִין עָלָיו מִלְמַעְלָה — "No man bruises his finger here on earth unless it was so decreed against him in Heaven" (*Chullin* 7b). Nothing ever occurs in the universe without the full will and consent of *Hashem*. Our reaction must be, as Maimonides teaches, to follow the path of *teshuvah* and constantly strive for spiritual improvement. We must be aware of our role as Jews and strengthen our observance of all aspects of the Torah.

The Talmud teaches: גְּדוֹלָה תְּשׁוּבָה שֶׁמְּקָרֶבֶת אֶת הַגְּאוּלָה שֶׁנֶּאֱמַר וּבָא לְצִיּוֹן גּוֹאֵל וּלְשָׁבֵי פֶשַׁע בְּיַעֲקֹב — "Repentance is so great that it hastens our redemption, as it is written, 'A redeemer shall come forth from Zion to those who repent from willful sin' '' (*Yoma* 86b). Let us hope and pray that because of the merits of repentance, *Hashem* will have mercy on His people, that He will remove us from distress to relief, from darkness to light, from subjugation to redemption with the coming of *Mashiach*, הַשְׁתָּא בַּעֲגָלָא וּבִזְמַן קָרִיב, speedily in our days.

Appendices

Appendix A*

The Death March
from Leipzig to Riesa

ERTRUD DEAK CAME FROM SZOMBATHY, hungary. She was born in a Jewish home for the elderly, where her father served as physician. When the Nazi Wehrmacht occupied Hungary in March 1944, her family was deported to Auschwitz, where her parents were murdered. Eventually, with the Russian advance into Poland, the concentration camp was evacuated and Gertrud was taken to Leipzig. The following is her report of the ensuing events:

---

*From notes written by Gertrud Deak in the Hungarian language. The German translation appeared in *Juden in Leipzig*. An English translation from the German follows.)

We were loaded onto freight train wagons and were told that we would be taken to Buchenwald. There was no food available for us, and because of constant bombardment by Allied planes, we were forced to stop our journey at regular intervals. On the second day, our transport came to a complete stop due to the destruction of the locomotive. Thirty-six hours later, another locomotive arrived. We were then informed that Buchenwald was no longer our destination, as the concentration camp had already been occupied by the American forces. Two days later, we arrived in Leipzig, where we were taken to an internment camp in the suburb of Thekla. At this camp we found 500 Hungarian women who had been there for several weeks. They had been brought there from somewhere near the Ostsee. They could not believe their eyes when they noticed our poor physical condition. They had been fortunate to have been interned under an unusually civil and courteous commandant who insisted on giving these women nourishing meals on a regular basis, their work obligations were extremely light, and all of them, too, were treated with kindness. We were given a most nourishing meal, we were able to shower, and were taken to unusually clean barracks where we were permitted to rest.

Approximately three hours after our arrival, low flying Allied bombers attacked the camp and within ten minutes, the entire camp was engulfed in flames. Apparently this camp was the headquarters for SS officers in the past, and the Allies were not aware of the fact that we, the victims of the Holocaust, were its present occupants. Our guards were able to utilize the shelters available at the camp during the bombardment but we had absolutely no protection. We were lying on the ground throughout the entire period of the air raid. I was holding the hand of my best friend when suddenly an object fell upon her and her head was crushed. I picked up the body of my best friend and ran with it to the hospital's pharmacy, although I knew quite well that she was dead. Finally the bombardment stopped. We remained in the camp in Leipzig-Thekla for several more days. As the advancing American troops reached the city's suburbs, the death march began. On that day many more people arrived. There were gypsies from the Ukraine, men and women from various camps, all in extremely poor physical condition. There were approximately 15,000 of us and we were lined up in rows of five. Our German guards loaded their baggage onto wagons that we were eventually forced to pull and the death march was under way. During the night, we were forced to walk barefoot in the snow. We received no nourishment. The guards shot everyone who, due to extreme physical exhaustion, stopped walking for a few moments. Occasionally, they would permit us to rest for two hours. Then the march would continue.

Under these dreadful and appalling conditions, our sole consolation was the sight of low-flying U.S. bombers who often made direct hits on our guards. Eventually, the guards began donning prisoners' jackets from the Buchenwald concentration camp to disguise themselves so that they might appear as victims to the pilots. During rest stops, the guards would hide beneath the wagons.

On the fourth day of the march, our row of five found a raw potato. We divided the potato into ten parts, each of us ate one part and saved the other for the following day. How delicious this tasted!

On the tenth day, we crossed the Elbe River near Klingenheim, somewhere between the cities of Riesa and Strehla. At this point, only 4,000 of us remained. Eleven thousand had perished during the march. The Germans brought two horses, killed them for us, cut them into small pieces, and threw them to us. To complete the meal, they added raw rice, which we gladly ate.

Meanwhile, low-flying Russian bombers conducted bombing raids in our vicinity. They flew so low that we could easily distinguish the pilots' faces. They bombed the entire area, circling around us, thus carefully avoiding inflicting any injuries to us. We were convinced that both the Americans and the Russians knew about our presence in the area and we were comforted by the knowledge that in a very short time we would be liberated and become free once again. Apparently, our guards also realized that the end was near. They decided that it would be safer for them to be taken prisoners by the Americans rather than the Russians. As a result, we were again organized into rows of five and we recrossed the Elbe River. We were now on its western bank, which was expected to be occupied by American troops. It must have been 5:30 a.m. when I awoke the following morning. Although, due to hunger, exhaustion, and extremely cold weather conditions, we were barely able to physically drag ourselves forward, nevertheless, a spark of human hope for survival still remained within us. I shall never forget the beautiful sunrise in the Duerer Landschaft that particular morning. It was the morning of my 21st birthday. I still was able to cross the bridge over the Elbe, but I could not possibly continue. Besides hunger and exhaustion, I suffered from dysentery. I broke down completely. This appeared to be the end of the line for me.

A guard immediately noticed my body on the ground. He kicked me with his boots several times and hit me sharply with his rifle butt. Since I was physically unable to react in any manner, he did not know how to deal with me. Finally, I heard him say, "She is not worth a bullet." He kicked me once more and continued marching with the group.

For many hours, I remained on the road covered with dirt. Then I began to crawl slowly. Two German women passed by and they were unusually friendly and compassionate. They suggested that I somehow drag myself to the nearest village which is a quarter of a mile away and take refuge in their barn. They promised to give me food at this barn. To remain on this road, they cautioned, was totally unsafe since many army vehicles were stationed in this zone. I followed their suggestion and literally crawled to the designated barn.

I was extremely terrified, when upon my arrival at the barn, I noticed a German army truck. But I soon realized that their prime concern was preparations to move to another station or to flee the area altogether. I then heard voices in the barn and attempted to hide. However, my fright turned to joy when I discovered that not only did they speak in Hungarian, but they were actually from my home town.

It was a mother and daughter who had succeeded in slipping into the barn when our group marched through the village. They were overjoyed to see me alive. They had been convinced that I was shot by the Nazi guard when I collapsed on the road. The two German women kept their promise and brought us food. However, they strongly urged us to move on when we finished our meal. The barn housed the army's horses and the Nazi soldiers could arrive at any moment.

So we left the barn. In a few minutes, we succeeded in discovering an empty warehouse, which became our new hiding place. It was awfully dark. We crawled into the straw we found and fell asleep . . .

Gertrud Deak was eventually liberated. After the war, she traveled to Paris and, being a professional kindergarten teacher, she was hired by a children's home in Montmorency, in the vicinity of Paris.

It should be noted that the distance covered in the ten-day death march from Leipzig to Riesa, in which more than 11,000 lost their lives, was approximately 80 kilometers, or 49 miles.

Appendix B

Leipzig's Synagogues

Gemeinde Synagogue — Gottschedstrasse 3

Eitz Chaim Synagogue — Otto Schill Strasse 8 (Apels Garten)

Talmud Torah Synagogue — Keilstrasse 4 (Broder Schul)

Ohel Yaakov Synagogue — Pfaffendorfer Strasse 4 (today Kurt Fischer Strasse)

Ahavath Torah Synagogue — Faerberstrasse 11

Beth Yehudah Synagogue — Faerberstrasse 11 (Ariowitsch Schul)

Chevra Mishnayoth Shul — Humboldtstrasse 24 (die Vierundzwanzig)

Tifereth Yehudah Shul — Eberhardtstrasse 11 (Bernstein Schul)

Tiktiner Shul — Bruehl 71 (later Richard Wagner Strasse 3)

Boyaner Shul — Leibnitzstrasse 24

Altersheim Shul — Auenstrasse

Bikur Cholim Shul — Eisenbahnstrasse 9 (today Ernst Thaelmann Strasse)

Bochnier Shul — Gerberstrasse 48-50

Yassyer Shul — Gerberstrasse 48-50

Krakauer Shul — Berliner Strasse

10 Lemberger Shul — address not known

Kolomeaer Shul — Berlinerstrasse 4

Shaare Zedek Synagogue — Schillerweg 31

Krochsiedlung Shul — Wilhelmshavener Strasse 2 — Leipzig, Gohlis

Aurelienstrasse Shul — Aurelienstrasse 14

BIBLIOGRAPHY

Field Enterprises Educational Corporation. *The World Book Encyclopedia*. Chicago, Illinois.

Hilberg, Raul. *The Destruction of the European Jews.*

Israelitische Religionsgemeinde. *Aus Geschichte und Leben der Juden in Leipzig.* Leipzig, Germany, 1930.

Keter Publishing House. *Encyclopaedia Judaica.* Jerusalem, Israel.

Levin, Nora. *The Holocaust.* 1973.

Rat des Bezirkes Leipzig. *Juden in Leipzig.* Leipzig, Germany, 1988.

Schwartz, Rabbi Yoel and Rabbi Yitzchak Goldstein, *Shoah.* Brooklyn, New York: Mesorah Publications, 1990.

Thalmann, Rita and Emmanuel Feinerman. *Crystal Night.* Paris, France, 1972.

Glossary

All entries are Hebrew unless otherwise noted: (G) German, (Y) Yiddish

Abend (G) — evening

Al Kiddush Hashem — for the sanctification of G-d's Name

Altersheim (G) — Old folks home

Anschluss (G) — annexation

Auf wiedersehn (G) — good bye

Bar Mitzvah — the age of 13 at which a Jewish male becomes obligated to observe the Torah's commandments

Ben Torah — one who studies and adheres to the teachings of the Torah

Bestecke (G) — silverware

Beth HaMidrash — house of worship and study

Betstube (G) — room used for prayer

Bimah — pulpit from where Torah is read

Bitte schoen (G) — you're welcome

Blatt (Y) — two sided-folio of the Talmud

Brachah (pl. brachos) — blessing

Chalef — knife used for slaughtering

Challah (pl. challos) — loaf of bread eaten on Shabbos

Chassidei umos haolam — the righteous among the nations of the world

Chassidic Rebbe — leader of a Chassidic sect

Chas veshalom — Heaven forbid

Chazzan — cantor

Chumash (pl. chumashim) — The five books of Moses

Churban — destruction

Danke schoen (G) — thank you

Daven (Y) — pray

Deena demalchusa deene — in monetary matters, Jewish law requires the observance of government regulations

Deutschland ueber alles (G) — Germany stands above all else

Dreckisch (er) (G) — filthy

Eretz Yisrael — the Land of Israel

Erev Shabbos — the day before Shabbos; Friday

Frau (G) — Mrs.

Friedhof (G) — cemetery

Gadlus — greatness

Galus — exile

Gadol (pl. gedolim) — prime Torah leader(s) of the generation

Gedolim — see *Gadol*

Gaon — outstanding Talmudic scholar

Gasse (G) — small street or alley

Gassus Haruach — arrogance

Gauleiter (G) — provincial leader

Gedenkt (G) — remember

Gemarah — Talmud; *seforim* which elaborate and interpret the Mishnah

Gemeinde (G) — community

Gemeindeblatt (G) — community newspaper

Gemeinderabbiner (G) — community Rabbi

Gemeindesynagoge (G) — community synagogue

Geschaeft (G) — store

Gestapo (G) — Nazi secret police

Guten Tag (G) — good day

Haggadah — text read on *Pesach* which relates the story the exodus from Egypt

Hakenkreuz (G) — swastika

Halachah (chic) — Jewish law

HaRav — the Rabbi

HaGaon — the eminent Talmudic scholar

Hashem — God

Hauptbahnhof (G) — main railroad station

Heil (G) — hail

Herr (G) — Mr.; Sir

Hitler Jugend (G) — Hitler's youth movement

Hochhaus (G) — skyscraper

Hoehere Israelitische Schule (G) — Advanced Jewish School

Jude (G) — Jew

Judenburg (G) — castle of Jews

Judengasse (G) — street of the Jews

Judenland (G) — land of the Jews

Judenstadt (G) — city of the Jews

Judenhaus (G) — house of the Jews

Judenrein (G) — a place empty of Jews

Judenstern (G) — Jewish star

Judenwohnungen (G) — Jewish residences

Juedisches Geschaeft (G) — Jewish place of business

Jugendhaus (G) — youth building

Kabbalah — rabbinic ordination for a ritual slaughterer

Kaffehaus (G) — coffee house; restuaurant

Kammerpaesse (G) — special passports issued to Jews

Kashrus — dietary laws

Kedoshim — people who have given their lives for the sanctification of God's name

Kehillah — community

Kitzur Shulchan Aruch — abridged version of the Code of Jewish Law

Koenig vom Bruehl (G) — nickname: king of the Bruehl (Bruehl is a street in Leipzig)

Kosher — food ritually permitted for consumption

Krankenhaus (G) — hospital

Kristallnacht (G) — night of broken glass

Kurfuerst (G) — a prince; sovereign

Lagerkomitee (G) — committee in charge of detainment camp

Lamdan — Torah scholar

Landsmannschaften (G) — society formed by individuals from the same community

Magen Dovid — the six-cornered Jewish star

Mark (G) — unit of German currency

Markgraf (G) — a military governor of a German province; a member of nobility

Mashiach — Messiah

Messe (G) — business fair

Mikvah — a body of water for ritual purification

Milchig (en) (Y) — dairy

Minyan — quorum of ten men required for prayer services

Mishnah (pl. mishnayos) — the codification of the oral law

Mitzvah (pl. mitzvos) — obligation instituted by the Torah or the Sages

Mohel — one who is ordained to perform circumcisions

Mussaf — additional prayer service for Sabbath and Holidays

Nach (G) — after; toward

Navi — Prophet

Oberbuergermeister (G) — mayor

Ohev Yisrael — one who loves Jews

Oneg Shabbos — lit. enjoyment of the Shabbos. A gathering on Shabbos with refreshments

Osten (G) — east

Ostjuden (G) — Jews from the east

Pasken (Y) — render a halachic decision

Pesach — Passover

Pikuach Nefesh — a situation where a life is endangered

Polizeiamtdirektor (G) — police director

Polizeipraesiduim (G) — police headquarters

Purim — Festival of Lots

Rachmanim — people who display mercy and compassion to others

Rashi — Acronym for **R Sh**lomo ben Isaac, a major commentator on the Bible

Rassenschaender (G) — desecrators of the race

Raus von Deutschland (G) — Get out of Germany

Rav (Rabbiner) — Rabbi

Reb — a respectful title preceding the name of a Jew; used in direct address

Rebbe (pl. *Rebbeim*) — 1. leader of group of Chassidim; 2. a Rabbi in his capacity as one's teacher

Reich (G) — empire

Reichsbankrat (G) — officer of government bank

Reichsgericht (G) — government court

Religionsgemeinde (G) — organized community of the members of a religious group

Rosh Hashanah — Jewish New Year

Rosh HaYeshivah — Head of the yeshivah

Schmutzig (er) (G) — dirty

Shul (G) — synagogue

Schule — school

Schule der Juden (G) — Jewish school

Schulmeister (G) — principal of a school

Schutzgeld (G) — money paid to be offered protection

Schutzjuden (G) — Jews who supervised activities of Jewish guests to Leipzig's fairs

Seder — religious ceremony on the first two nights of Passover

Sefer (pl. *Seforim*) — book

Schwanenteich (G) — pond for swans and ducks

Shabbos — Sabbath

Shailah — question on Jewish law

Shechitah — ritual slaughtering

Shechunah — neighborhood

Shiur (pl. shiurim) — lecture or class on a Jewish topic

Shochet (pl. shochtim) — ritual slaughterer

Shtibel (pl. shtiblach) — small synagogue

Shulchan Aruch — Code of the Jewish Law

Siddur — prayerbook

Semichah — Rabbinic degree

Statenlos (G) — stateless

Strasse (G) — street

Succah — a booth (Jews are obligated to dwell in one on Succos)

Succos — Holiday of Tabernacles

Tageblatt (G) — daily newspaper

Talmid Chacham — a Torah scholar

Talmud — Gemarah; it elaborates on the Mishnah in great detail

Talmud Torah — an elementary school for Torah studies

Tannah — a scholar of the Talmudic era

Tante (G) — aunt

Teshuvah — repentance

Tochachah (pl. Tochachos) — reproof(s)

Tod (G) — death

Torah — five books of Moses

Treif — not ritually fit for consumption

Tza'ar ba'alei chaim — cruelty to animals

Tzaddik — righteous person

Unerwuenscht (G) — not wanted

Unglueck (G) — misfortune

Verein (G) — organization

Verflucht (er) (G) — cursed (one)

Vierundzwanzig (G) — twenty-four

Vom (G) — from

Vorsitzender (G) — chairman

Vorstand (G) — Board of Directors

Wehrmacht (G) — German army

Yemach Shemo — may his name be erased

Yeshivah (pl. yeshivos) — Academy where Torah and is taught

Yeshivos Ketanos — day schools on the elementary level

Yiddish (Y) — Jewish

Yiddishkeit (Y) — Judaism

Yom Kippur — Day of Atonement

Yom Tov (pl. Yomim Tovim) — holiday(s)

Zachor — remember

Zwangseinweisung in Jedenwohnungen (G) — forced moving of Jews to special residences

This volume is part of
THE ARTSCROLL SERIES®
an ongoing project of
translations, commentaries and expositions
on Scripture, Mishnah, Talmud, liturgy,
history, the classic Rabbinic writings,
biographies, and thought.

For a brochure of current publications
visit your local Hebrew bookseller
or contact the publisher:

Mesorah Publications, ltd

4401 Second Avenue
Brooklyn, New York 11232
(718) 921-9000